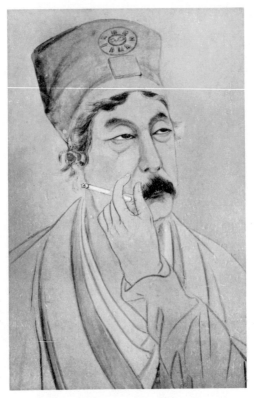

Okakura Kakuzo by Shimomura Kanzan

THE BOOK
OF TEA

by Okakura Kakuzo

with
Foreword & Biographical Sketch
by Elise Grilli

CHARLES E. TUTTLE COMPANY
Rutland, Vermont—Tokyo, Japan

Published by the Charles E. Tuttle Company
of Rutland, Vermont & Tokyo, Japan
with editorial offices at 15 Edogawa-cho,
Bunkyo-ku, Tokyo, Japan by arrangement
with Dodd, Mead & Company, Inc., N. Y.

Library of Congress Catalog
Card No. 56–13134

Originally published, 1906

Tuttle edition

First printing, 1956
Sixth printing, 1960

Typography and book design by Kaoru Ogimi

Printed in Japan by the Toppan Printing Company, Tokyo

CONTENTS

NOTE ON THE ILLUSTRATIONS

The Frontispiece is reproduced from a preliminary sketch for a portrait by Shimomura Kanzan, one of Okakura's outstanding pupils, and is used here by the kind permission of the Geijutsu University and Mr. Hidetoki Shimomura, Kanzan's grandson. The sketch, in Japanese ink and traces of water colors on paper, mounted as a hanging scroll, was formerly in the possession of Mr. Langdon Warner, of Harvard University, who returned it to Japan after the finished portrait was destroyed in the Great Earthquake of 1923. The rather conspicuous errors in draftsmanship, particularly noticeable in the hand holding the cigarette, were corrected in the final painting, which was one of Kanzan's masterpieces.

The illustrations at the head of each chapter are taken from the ink drawings of Sesshu (1420–1506), the greatest of all Japanese painters in the same Zen tradition which inspired the tea ceremony.

FOREWORD

by Elise Grilli

NOT ALWAYS does the fame of an author keep step with the fame of his books. Sometimes the man advances and his work recedes, as, for example, in the case of Dr. Samuel Johnson, whose personality continues to intrigue us today, just as much as it did his contemporaries; we can still see him vividly through the eyes of Boswell and other diarists and recorders, while much of his own writing has taken on an obsolescent tinge.

The opposite fate seems to have befallen Okakura Kakuzo and *The Book of Tea*. The book is just fifty years old, and in this half century its fame has grown steadily and continuously. Starting out as an esoteric morsel for a select few in the small aesthetic world of Boston at the turn of the century, it has been moving in ever-widening circles, propelled as by a natural movement across the waters that lap the shores of Asia and of Europe, always radiating from the modest little edition that first appeared in America in 1906. From this original publication in English, the book has been translated into innumerable languages including, as an ironical apogee of fame, its author's native tongue, Japanese. Its sales through the years and in many languages and editions reach certainly into the hundreds of thousands, and nothing bears more eloquent witness to its continuing appeal than that it should now be appearing in this present new and handsome edition.

Yet the name of the book's author is becoming dimmer with the years even in Japan —or, rather, especially in Japan, where today he merits only a short paragraph in the national biographical dictionary. As important as the book is, Okakura deserves much more than to be remembered merely as the author of *The Book of Tea*. For his accomplishments were great and his stature large. Now, more than forty years after his death, his memory still remains vivid for his one-time students and collaborators. For them he was a Character, with a capital *C*, and a genius, at least with a small *g*. As one talks with those who remember him it becomes clear that his striking appearance and dramatic personality could not possibly be forgotten by anyone who came into contact with him.

As may be seen in the biographical sketch appended to this volume, his was not the old story of the prophet who had to be recognized by the world at large before he could be acknowledged in his own land. Quite the contrary. For some two decades, from 1880 to 1900, Okakura stood at the very center of Japan's art activities. He was a key figure in the gigantic effort to bring some order into the cataclysmic clash between Oriental tradition and Western innovation, which shook Japan to its very foundations. That very prominence, however, exposed some of the leaders to the inevitable series of attacks and intrigues of smaller men who were envious and quarrelsome and eager to topple the giants from their heights.

This situation was aggravated by Okakura's own pronouncements, for he possessed in no small measure "the gentle art of making enemies." In appearance, in speech, and in demeanor he was the *grand seigneur,* as well as the crusader imbued with the righteousness of his cause. Of such stuff were many of the men who stood by the Emperor Meiji in the early years of Japan's awakening after her long sleep of medievalism; but by the year 1900 the heroic was giving way to the picayune, and Okakura could not adjust himself to the smaller vision. He sought and found a response in the world beyond Japan's frontiers, traveling extensively in India, China, and Europe, and finally finding his niche as Curator of Oriental Art at the Boston Museum, where, as his star rose in the West, it declined in the East.

Okakura's literary works have, to some

extent, been superceded by the later, more systematic approach to the study of Oriental art, for which he himself prepared the way. The same fate has overtaken the writings of Ernest Fenollosa, for both these men were pioneers who planned wide vistas and then left the minutiae to more scientific writers. It would be carping to follow in their footsteps today and point out errors here and there. The enthusiasm of these men was incendiary, and without their spark the whole chemical reaction might have remained dormant for many years—perhaps too late to make use of the fragile raw material. Their prime function was to preserve a whole body of art from possible extinction. If in addition, they had poetic insight and a contagious enthusiasm, the gods have been kind enough.

Okakura's writings range from historical enumeration to poetic fantasy, and from philosophic speculation to nationalistic apologia. For the Japanese periodical *Kokka,* which had been founded in 1889, he contributed numerous articles on art-historical themes. *The Ideals of the East* may seem a bit vaporous for today's taste, and *The Awakening of Japan* has also been replaced by more factual writing, though some of its thoughts are still being quoted and paraphrased by later writers. The poems which he dedicated directly to Mrs. Isabella Gardner have remained too personal for wider circulation, nor has that lady's enthusiasm for his fairy drama with music, entitled *The White Fox,* brought that work to life on the operatic stage. His *Historical Notes on Japanese Temples and Their Treasures* made a substantial contribution to this field and has survived emendations and revisions. But it is *The Book of Tea* that seems to be most richly endowed with an elixir of life, which has kept it youthful and vigorous for half a century.

Okakura wrote *The Book of Tea* soon after his arrival in America, and before publication he read it aloud in the artistic gatherings that centered around Mrs. Gardner, the "Queen of Boston," who ruled over an aesthetic kingdom in her palatial home at Fenway Court. Apparently the book was intended for a narrow elite, who might be expected to join in his protest against the spiritual misunderstandings that separated East and West. The rest of the world, the author seemed to think, would very likely consider his theme a sort of tempest in a teacup:

"The average Westerner, in his sleek complacency, will see in the tea ceremony but another instance of the thousand and one oddities which constitute the quaintness and the childishness of the East to him. . . ."

Yet the book continues to be passed from hand to hand, always with the previous reader's warm assurance that here is to be found a key to an understanding of Eastern ideas, a key that transcends the title of the book. Okakura's insight and compassion, his irony and his power of self-observation, and the piquant lyricism of his style have won the book a far greater audience than he could ever have imagined. His felicitous phrasing and dramatic presentation of his theme first arouse curiosity in the reader, then interest, and finally a desire for comprehension and participation. Later writings by other men may have presented the tea cult of Japan in a more objective light, but Okakura revealed to the West a unified concept of art and life, of nature and art blended into a harmony of daily living, which strikes a responsive chord in a world anxious to find a way out from the maze of complexities into which it has blundered.

The past fifty years have removed some of the mutual ignorance between the continents that Okakura had observed with bitterness. There has been a decided decline in colonial paternalism and a rise in the respect with which the East and the West regard each other's cultural patterns and ancient wisdoms. It may be too presumptuous and too optimistic to attribute much of the *rapprochement* to a mild little volume like *The Book of Tea* or to the literature that has grown up after its publication; it may also be necessary to admit that the very wars which Okakura feared and detested have contributed in a horribly bloody way to a remarkable realization that East and West are not so far apart, after all. In any case, Okakura today would be astonished at the extent to which "humanity has met in a teacup."

Tokyo, July, 1956

✻ THE BOOK OF TEA ✻

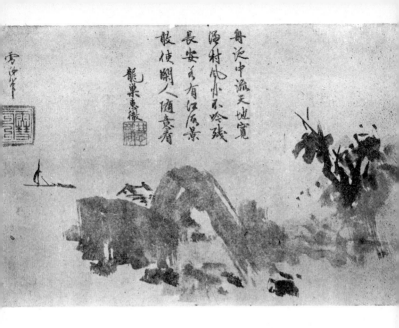

THE CUP OF HUMANITY

TEA BEGAN as a medicine and grew into a beverage. In China, in the eighth century, it entered the realm of poetry as one of the polite amusements. The fifteenth century saw Japan ennoble it into a religion of aestheticism—Teaism. Teaism is a cult founded on the adoration of the beautiful among the sordid facts of everyday existence.

It inculcates purity and harmony, the mystery of mutual charity, the romanticism of the social order. It is essentially a worship of the Imperfect, as it is a tender attempt to accomplish something possible in this impossible thing we know as life.

The Philosophy of Tea is not mere aestheticism in the ordinary acceptance of the term, for it expresses conjointly with ethics and religion our whole point of view about man and nature. It is hygiene, for it enforces cleanliness; it is economics, for it shows comfort in simplicity rather than in the complex and costly; it is moral geometry, inasmuch as it defines our sense of proportion to the universe. It represents the true spirit of Eastern democracy by making all its votaries aristocrats in taste.

The long isolation of Japan from the rest of the world, so conducive to introspection, has been highly favourable to the development of Teaism. Our home and habits, costume and cuisine, porcelain, lacquer, painting—our very literature—all have been

4

subject to its influence. No student of Japanese culture could ever ignore its presence. It has permeated the elegance of noble boudoirs, and entered the abode of the humble. Our peasants have learned to arrange flowers, our meanest labourer to offer his salutation to the rocks and waters. In our common parlance we speak of the man "with no tea" in him, when he is insusceptible to the serio-comic interests of the personal drama. Again we stigmatise the untamed aesthete who, regardless of the mundane tragedy, runs riot in the springtide of emancipated emotions, as one "with too much tea" in him.

The outsider may indeed wonder at this seeming much ado about nothing. What a tempest in a tea-cup! he will say. But when we consider how small after all the cup of human enjoyment is, how soon overflowed with tears, how easily drained to the dregs in our quenchless thirst for infinity, we shall not blame ourselves for making so much of the tea-cup. Mankind has done worse. In the worship of Bacchus, we have sacrificed too freely; and we have even transfigured the gory image of Mars. Why not consecrate ourselves to the queen of the Camelias, and revel in the warm stream of sympathy that flows from her altar? In the liquid amber within the ivory-porcelain, the initiated may touch the sweet reticence of Confucius, the piquancy of Laotse, and the ethereal aroma of Sakyamuni himself.

Those who cannot feel the littleness of great things in themselves are apt to overlook the greatness of little things in others. The average Westerner, in his sleek complacency, will see in the tea ceremony but another instance of the thousand and one oddities which constitute the quaintness and childishness of the East to him. He was wont to regard Japan as barbarous while she indulged in the gentle arts of peace: he calls her civilised since she began to commit wholesale slaughter on Manchurian battlefields. Much comment has been given lately to the Code of the Samurai,—the Art of Death

6

which makes our soldiers exult in self-sacri-
fice; but scarcely any attention has been
drawn to Teaism, which represents so much
of our Art of Life. Fain would we remain
barbarians, if our claim to civilisation were
to be based on the gruesome glory of war.
Fain would we await the time when due
respect shall be paid to our art and ideals.

When will the West understand, or try
to understand, the East? We Asiatics are
often appalled by the curious web of facts
and fancies which has been woven concerning us. We are pictured as living on the per-
fume of the lotus, if not on mice and cock-
roaches. It is either impotent fanaticism or
else abject voluptuousness. Indian spirituality
has been derided as ignorance, Chinese so-
briety as stupidity, Japanese patriotism as the
result of fatalism. It has been said that we
are less sensible to pain and wounds on
account of the callousness of our nervous
organisation!

Why not amuse yourselves at our expense?
Asia returns the compliment. There would

be further food for merriment if you were
to know all that we have imagined and
written about you. All the glamour of the
perspective is there, all the unconscious
homage of wonder, all the silent resentment
of the new and undefined. You have been
loaded with virtues too refined to be envied,
and accused of crimes too picturesque to be
condemned. Our writers in the past—the
wise men who knew—informed us that you
had bushy tails somewhere hidden in your
garments, and often dined off a fricassée of
newborn babes! Nay, we had something
worse against you: we used to think you the
most impracticable people on the earth, for
you were said to preach what you never
practised.

Such misconceptions are fast vanishing
amongst us. Commerce has forced the European tongues on many an Eastern port.
Asiatic youths are flocking to Western col-
leges for the equipment of modern education. Our insight does not penetrate your
culture deeply, but at least we are willing to

learn. Some of my compatriots have adopted too much of your customs and too much of your etiquette, in the delusion that the acquisition of stiff collars and tall silk hats comprised the attainment of your civilisation. Pathetic and deplorable as such affectations are, they evince our willingness to approach the West on our knees. Unfortunately the Western attitude is unfavourable to the understanding of the East. The Christian missionary goes to impart, but not to receive. Your information is based on the meagre translations of our immense literature, if not on the unreliable anecdotes of passing travellers. It is rarely that the chivalrous pen of a Lafcadio Hearn or that of the author of "The Web of Indian Life" enlivens the Oriental darkness with the torch of our own sentiments.

Perhaps I betray my own ignorance of the Tea Cult by being so outspoken. Its very spirit of politeness exacts that you say what you are expected to say, and no more. But I am not to be a polite Teaist. So much harm has been done already by the mutual misunderstanding of the New World and the Old, that one need not apologise for contributing his tithe to the furtherance of a better understanding. The beginning of the twentieth century would have been spared the spectacle of sanguinary warfare if Russia had condescended to know Japan better. What dire consequences to humanity lie in the contemptuous ignoring of Eastern problems! European imperialism, which does not disdain to raise the absurd cry of the Yellow Peril, fails to realise that Asia may also awaken to the cruel sense of the White Disaster. You may laugh at us for having "too much tea," but may we not suspect that you of the West have "no tea" in your constitution?

Let us stop the continents from hurling epigrams at each other, and be sadder if not wiser by the mutual gain of half a hemisphere. We have developed along different lines, but there is no reason why one should not supplement the other. You have gained expansion at the cost of restlessness; we have created a harmony which is weak against aggression. Will you believe it?—the East is better off in some respects than the West!

Strangely enough humanity has so far met in the tea-cup. It is the only Asiatic ceremonial which commands universal esteem. The white man has scoffed at our religion and our morals, but has accepted the brown beverage without hesitation. The afternoon tea is now an important function in Western society. In the delicate clatter of trays and saucers, in the soft rustle of feminine hospitality, in the common catechism about cream and sugar, we know that the Worship of Tea is established beyond question. The philosophic resignation of the guest to the fate awaiting him in the dubious decoction proclaims that in this single instance the Oriental spirit reigns supreme.

The earliest record of tea in European writing is said to be found in the statement of an Arabian traveller, that after the year

879 the main sources of revenue in Canton were the duties on salt and tea. Marco Polo records the deposition of a Chinese minister of finance in 1285 for his arbitrary augmentation of the tea-taxes. It was at the period of the great discoveries that the European people began to know more about the extreme Orient. At the end of the sixteenth century the Hollanders brought the news that a pleasant drink was made in the East from the leaves of a bush. The travellers Giovanni Batista Ramusio (1559), L. Almeida (1576), Maffeno (1588), Tareira (1610), also mentioned tea. In the last-named year ships of the Dutch East India Company brought the first tea into Europe. It was known in France in 1636, and reached Russia in 1638. England welcomed it in 1650 and spoke of it as "That excellent and by all physicians approved China drink, called by the Chineans Tcha, and by other nations Tay, alias Tee."

Like all the good things of the world, the propaganda of Tea met with opposition. Heretics like Henry Saville (1678) denounced drinking it as a filthy custom. Jonas Hanway (Essay on Tea, 1756) said that men seemed to lose their stature and comeliness, women their beauty through the use of tea. Its cost at the start (about fifteen or sixteen shillings a pound) forbade popular consumption, and made it "regalia for high treatments and entertainments, presents being made thereof to princes and grandees." Yet in spite of such drawbacks tea-drinking spread with marvellous rapidity. The coffee-houses of London in the early half of the eighteenth century became, in fact, tea-houses, the resort of wits like Addison and Steele, who beguiled themselves over their "dish of tea." The beverage soon became a necessary of life—a taxable matter. We are reminded in this connection what an important part it plays in modern history. Colonial America resigned herself to oppression until human endurance gave way before the heavy duties laid on Tea. American independence dates from the throwing of tea-chests into Boston harbour.

There is a subtle charm in the taste of tea which makes it irresistible and capable of idealisation. Western humourists were not slow to mingle the fragrance of their thought with its aroma. It has not the arrogance of wine, the self-consciousness of coffee, nor the simpering innocence of cocoa. Already in 1711, says the Spectator: "I would therefore in a particular manner recommend these my speculations to all well-regulated families that set apart an hour every morning for tea, bread and butter; and would earnestly advise them for their good to order this paper to be punctually served up and to be looked upon as a part of the tea-equipage." Samuel Johnson draws his own portrait as "a hardened and shameless tea-drinker, who for twenty years diluted his meals with only the infusion of the fascinating plant; who with tea amused the evening, with tea solaced the midnight, and with tea welcomed the morning."

Charles Lamb, a professed devotee, sounded the true note of Teaism when he wrote that the greatest pleasure he knew was to do a good action by stealth, and to have it found out by accident. For Teaism is the art of concealing beauty that you may discover it, of suggesting what you dare not reveal. It is the noble secret of laughing at yourself, calmly yet thoroughly, and is thus humour itself,—the smile of philosophy. All genuine humourists may in this sense be called tea-philosophers,—Thackeray, for instance, and, of course, Shakespeare. The poets of the Decadence (when was not the world in decadence?), in their protests against materialism, have, to a certain extent, also opened the way to Teaism. Perhaps nowadays it is in our demure contemplation of the Imperfect that the West and the East can meet in mutual consolation.

The Taoists relate that at the great beginning of the No-Beginning, Spirit and Matter met in mortal combat. At last the Yellow Emperor, the Sun of Heaven, triumphed over Shuhyung, the demon of darkness and earth. The Titan, in his death agony, struck his head against the solar vault and shivered the blue dome of jade into fragments. The stars lost their nests, the moon wandered aimlessly among the wild chasms of the night. In despair the Yellow Emperor sought far and wide for the repairer of the Heavens. He had not to search in vain. Out of the Eastern sea rose a queen, the divine Niuka, horn-crowned and dragon-tailed, resplendent in her armour of fire. She welded the five-coloured rainbow in her magic cauldron and rebuilt the Chinese sky. But it is also told that Niuka forgot to fill two tiny crevices in the blue firmament. Thus began the dualism of love—two souls rolling through space and never at rest until they join together to complete the universe. Everyone has to build anew his sky of hope and peace.

The heaven of modern humanity is indeed shattered in the Cyclopean struggle for wealth and power. The world is groping in the shadow of egotism and vulgarity. Knowledge is bought through a bad conscience, benevolence practised for the sake of utility.

16

The East and West, like two dragons tossed in a sea of ferment, in vain strive to regain the jewel of life. We need a Niuka again to repair the grand devastation; we await the great Avatar. Meanwhile, let us have a sip of tea. The afternoon glow is brightening the bamboos, the fountains are bubbling with delight, the soughing of the pines is heard in our kettle. Let us dream of evanescence, and linger in the beautiful foolishness of things.

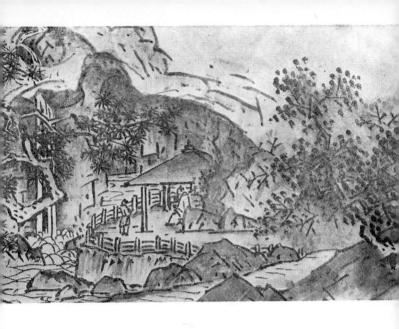

THE SCHOOLS OF TEA

T EA IS a work of art and needs a master hand to bring out its noblest qualities. We have good and bad tea, as we have good and bad paintings—generally the latter. There is no single recipe for making the perfect tea, as there are no rules for producing a Titian or a Sesson. Each preparation of the leaves has its individuality, its special

affinity with water and heat, its hereditary
memories to recall, its own method of telling
a story. The truly beautiful must be always
in it. How much do we not suffer through
the constant failure of society to recognise
this simple and fundamental law of art and
life; Lichihlai, a Sung poet, has sadly remarked that there were three most deplorable
things in the world: the spoiling of fine
youths through false education, the degrada-
tion of fine paintings through vulgar admiration, and the utter waste of fine tea through
incompetent manipulation.

Like Art, Tea has its periods and its
schools. Its evolution may be roughly divided
into three main stages: the Boiled Tea, the
Whipped Tea, and the Steeped Tea. We
moderns belong to the last school. These
several methods of appreciating the beverage
are indicative of the spirit of the age in which
they prevailed. For life is an expression, our
unconscious actions the constant betrayal of
our innermost thought. Confucius said that
"man hideth not." Perhaps we reveal our-

selves too much in small things because we
have so little of the great to conceal. The tiny
incidents of daily routine are as much a com-
mentary of racial ideals as the highest flight
of philosophy or poetry. Even as the difference in favourite vintage marks the separate
idiosyncrasies of different periods and nation-
alities of Europe, so the Tea-ideals character-
ise the various moods of Oriental culture.
The Cake-tea which was boiled, the Pow-
dered-tea which was whipped, the Leaf-
tea which was steeped, mark the distinct
emotional impulses of the Tang, the Sung,
and the Ming dynasties of China. If
we were inclined to borrow the much-
abused terminology of art classification, we
might designate them respectively, the
Classic, the Romantic, and the Naturalistic
schools of Tea.

The tea-plant, a native of southern China,
was known from very early times to Chinese
botany and medicine. It is alluded to in the
classics under the various names of Tou,
Tseh, Chung, Kha, and Ming, and was

highly prized for possessing the virtues of relieving fatigue, delighting the soul, strengthening the will, and repairing the eyesight. It was not only administered as an internal dose, but often applied externally in form of paste to alleviate rheumatic pains. The Taoists claimed it as an important ingredient of the elixir of immortality. The Buddhists used it extensively to prevent drowsiness during their long hours of meditation.

By the fourth and fifth centuries Tea became a favourite beverage among the inhabitants of the Yangtse-Kiang valley. It was about this time that the modern ideograph Cha was coined, evidently a corruption of the classic Tou. The poets of the southern dynasties have left some fragments of their fervent adoration of the "froth of the liquid jade." Then emperors used to bestow some rare preparation of the leaves on their high ministers as a reward for eminent services. Yet the method of drinking tea at this stage was primitive in the extreme. The leaves

22

were steamed, crushed in a mortar, made into a cake, and boiled together with rice, ginger, salt, orange peel, spices, milk, and sometimes with onions! The custom obtains at the present day among the Thibetans and various Mongolian tribes, who make a curious syrup of these ingredients. The use of lemon slices by the Russians, who learned to take tea from the Chinese caravansaries, points to the survival of the ancient method.

It needed the genius of the Tang dynasty to emancipate Tea from its crude state and lead to its final idealisation. With Luwuh in the middle of the eighth century we have our first apostle of tea. He was born in an age when Buddhism, Taoism, and Confucianism were seeking mutual synthesis. The pantheistic symbolism of the time was urging one to mirror the Universal in the Particular. Luwuh, a poet, saw in the Tea-service the same harmony and order which reigned through all things. In his celebrated work, the "Chaking" (The Holy Scripture of Tea) he formulated the Code of Tea. He has since been worshipped as the tutelary god of the Chinese tea merchants.

The "Chaking" consists of three volumes and ten chapters. In the first chapter Luwuh treats of the nature of the tea-plant, in the second of the implements for gathering the leaves, in the third of the selection of the leaves. According to him the best quality of the leaves must have "creases like the leathern boot of Tartar horsemen, curl like the dewlap of a mighty bullock, unfold like a mist rising out of a ravine, gleam like a lake touched by a zephyr, and be wet and soft like fine earth newly swept by rain."

The fourth chapter is devoted to the enumeration and description of the twenty-four members of the tea-equipage, beginning with the tripod brazier and ending with the bamboo cabinet for containing all these utensils. Here we notice Luwuh's predilection for Taoist symbolism. Also it is interesting to observe in this connection the influence of tea on Chinese ceramics. The Celestial porcelain, as is well known, had its origin in an attempt to reproduce the exquisite shade of jade, resulting, in the Tang dynasty, in the blue glaze of the south, and the white glaze of the north. Luwuh considered the blue as the ideal colour for the tea-cup, as it lent additional greenness to the beverage, whereas the white made it look pinkish and distasteful. It was because he used cake-tea. Later on, when the tea-masters of Sung took to the powdered tea, they preferred heavy bowls of blue-black and dark brown. The Mings, with their steeped tea, rejoiced in light ware of white porcelain.

In the fifth chapter Luwuh describes the method of making tea. He eliminates all ingredients except salt. He dwells also on the much-discussed question of the choice of water and the degree of boiling it. According to him, the mountain spring is the best, the river water and the spring water come next in the order of excellence. There are three stages of boiling: the first boil is when the little bubbles like the eye of fishes swim on the surface; the second boil is when the bubbles are like crystal beads rolling in a fountain; the third boil is when the billows surge wildly in the kettle. The Cake-tea is roasted before the fire until it becomes soft like a baby's arm and is shredded into powder between pieces of fine paper. Salt is put in the first boil, the tea in the second. At the third boil, a dipperful of cold water is poured into the kettle to settle the tea and revive the "youth of the water." Then the beverage was poured into cups and drunk. O nectar! The filmy leaflet hung like scaly clouds in a serene sky or floated like water-lilies on emerald streams. It was of such a beverage that Lotung, a Tang poet, wrote: "The first cup moistens my lips and throat, the second cup breaks my loneliness, the third cup searches my barren entrail but to find therein some five thousand volumes of odd ideographs. The fourth cup raises a slight perspiration, — all the wrong of life passes away through my pores. At the fifth cup I am purified; the sixth cup calls me to the realms of immortals. The seventh cup—ah, but I could take no more! I only feel the breath of cool wind that rises in my sleeves. Where is Horaisan? Let me ride on this sweet breeze and waft away thither."

The remaining chapters of the "Chaking" treat of the vulgarity of the ordinary methods of tea-drinking, a historical summary of illustrious tea-drinkers, the famous tea plantations of China, the possible variations of the tea-service, and illustrations of the tea-utensils. The last is unfortunately lost.

The appearance of the "Chaking" must have created considerable sensation at the time. Luwuh was befriended by the Emperor Taisung (763–779), and his fame attracted many followers. Some exquisites were said to have been able to detect the tea made by Luwuh from that of his disciples. One mandarin has his name immortalised by his failure to appreciate the tea of this great master.

In the Sung dynasty the whipped tea came into fashion and created the second school of Tea. The leaves were ground to fine pow-

der in a small stone mill, and the preparation was whipped in hot water by a delicate
whisk made of split bamboo. The new process led to some change in the tea-equipage
of Luwuh, as well as the choice of leaves.
Salt was discarded forever. The enthusiasm
of the Sung people for tea knew no bounds.
Epicures vied with each other in discovering
new varieties, and regular tournaments were
held to decide their superiority. The Emperor Kiasung (1101–1124), who was too
great an artist to be a well-behaved monarch,
lavished his treasures on the attainment of
rare species. He himself wrote a dissertation
on the twenty kinds of tea, among which he
prizes the "white tea" as of the rarest and
finest quality.

The tea-ideal of the Sungs differed from
the Tangs even as their notion of life differed. They sought to actualise what their
predecessors tried to symbolise. To the Neo-
Confucian mind the cosmic law was not re-
flected in the phenomenal world, but the
phenomenal world was the cosmic law itself.

28

Æons were but moments—Nirvana always within grasp. The Taoist conception that immortality lay in the eternal change permeated all their modes of thought. It was the process, not the deed, which was interesting. It was the completing, not the completion, which was really vital. Man came thus at once face to face with nature. A new meaning grew into the art of life. The tea began to be not a poetical pastime, but one of the methods of self-realisation. Wangyucheng eulogised tea as "flooding his soul like a direct appeal, that its delicate bitterness reminded him of the after-taste of a good counsel." Sotumpa wrote of the strength of the immaculate purity in tea which defied corruption as a truly virtuous man. Among the Buddhists, the southern Zen sect, which incorporated so much of Taoist doctrines, formulated an elaborate ritual of tea. The monks gathered before the image of Bodhi Dharma and drank tea out of a single bowl with the profound formality of a holy sacrament. It was this Zen ritual which finally developed into the Tea-ceremony of Japan in the fifteenth century.

Unfortunately the sudden outburst of the Mongol tribes in the thirteenth century, which resulted in the devastation and conquest of China under the barbaric rule of the Yuen Emperors, destroyed all the fruits of Sung culture. The native dynasty of the Mings which attempted re-nationalisation in the middle of the fifteenth century was harassed by internal troubles, and China again fell under the alien rule of the Manchus in the seventeenth century. Manners and customs changed to leave no vestige of the former times. The powdered tea is entirely forgotten. We find a Ming commentator at loss to recall the shape of the tea whisk mentioned in one of the Sung classics. Tea is now taken by steeping the leaves in hot water in a bowl or cup. The reason why the Western world is innocent of the older method of drinking tea is explained by the fact that Europe knew it only at the close of the Ming dynasty.

To the latter-day Chinese tea is a delicious

beverage, but not an ideal. The long woes of his country have robbed him of the zest for the meaning of life. He has become modern, that is to say, old and disenchanted. He has lost that sublime faith in illusions which constitutes the eternal youth and vigour of the poets and ancients. He is an eclectic and politely accepts the traditions of the universe. He toys with Nature, but does not condescend to conquer or worship her. His Leaf-tea is often wonderful with its flower-like aroma, but the romance of the Tang and Sung ceremonials are not to be found in his cup.

Japan, which followed closely on the footsteps of Chinese civilisation, has known the tea in all its three stages. As early as the year 729 we read of the Emperor Shomu giving tea to one hundred monks at his palace in Nara. The leaves were probably imported by our ambassadors to the Tang Court and prepared in the way then in fashion. In 801 the monk Saicho brought back some seeds and planted them in Yeisan. Many tea-gardens

31

are heard of in the succeeding centuries, as well as the delight of the aristocracy and priesthood in the beverage. The Sung tea reached us in 1191 with the return of Yeisai-zenji, who went there to study the southern Zen school. The new seeds which he carried home were successfully planted in three places, one of which, the Uji district near Kioto, bears still the name of producing the best tea in the world. The southern Zen spread with marvellous rapidity, and with it the tea-ritual and the tea-ideal of the Sung. By the fifteenth century, under the patronage of the Shogun, Ashikaga-Yoshimasa, the tea ceremony is fully constituted and made into an independent and secular performance. Since then Teaism is fully established in Japan. The use of the steeped tea of the later China is comparatively recent among us, being only known since the middle of the seventeenth century. It has replaced the pow-dered tea in ordinary consumption, though the latter still continues to hold its place as the tea of teas.

It is in the Japanese tea ceremony that we see the culmination of tea-ideals. Our successful resistance of the Mongol invasion in 1281 had enabled us to carry on the Sung movement so disastrously cut off in China itself through the nomadic inroad. Tea with us became more than an idealisation of the form of drinking; it is a religion of the art of life. The beverage grew to be an excuse for the worship of purity and refinement, a sacred function at which the host and guest joined to produce for that occasion the utmost beatitude of the mundane. The tea-room was an oasis in the dreary waste of existence where weary travellers could meet to drink from the common spring of art-appreciation. The ceremony was an improvised drama whose plot was woven about the tea, the flowers, and the paintings. Not a colour to disturb the tone of the room, not a sound to mar the rhythm of things, not a gesture to obtrude on the harmony, not a word to break the unity of the surroundings, all movements to be performed simply and naturally—such

33

were the aims of the tea-ceremony. And strangely enough it was often successful. A subtle philosophy lay behind it all. Teaism was Taoism in disguise.

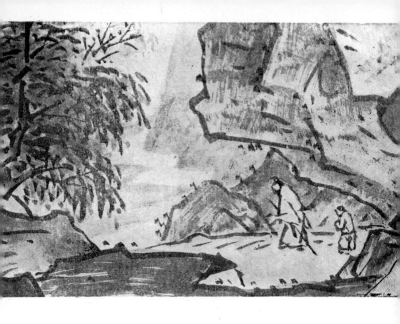

TAOISM AND ZENNISM

THE CONNECTION of Zennism with tea is proverbial. We have already remarked that the tea-ceremony was a development of the Zen ritual. The name of Laotse, the founder of Taoism, is also intimately associated with the history of tea. It is written in the Chinese school manual concerning the origin of habits and customs that the ceremony of offering tea to a guest began with Kwanyin, a well-known disciple of Laotse, who first at the gate of the Han Pass presented to the "Old Philosopher" a cup of the golden elixir. We shall not stop to discuss the authenticity of such tales, which are valuable, however, as confirming the early use of the beverage by the Taoists. Our interest in Taoism and Zennism here lies mainly in those ideas regarding life and art which are so embodied in what we call Teaism.

It is to be regretted that as yet there appears to be no adequate presentation of the Taoist and Zen doctrines in any foreign language, though we have had several laudable attempts.

Translation is always a treason, and as a Ming author observes, can at its best be only the reverse side of a brocade,—all the threads are there, but not the subtlety of colour or design. But, after all, what great doctrine is there which is easy to expound? The ancient sages never put their teachings in systematic form. They spoke in paradoxes, for they were afraid of uttering half-truths. They began by talking like fools and ended by making their hearers wise. Laotse himself, with his quaint humour, says, "If people of inferior intelligence hear of the Tao, they laugh immensely. It would not be the Tao unless they laughed at it."

The Tao literally means a Path. It has been severally translated as the Way, the Absolute, the Law, Nature, Supreme Reason, the Mode. These renderings are not incorrect, for the use of the term by the Taoists differs according to the subject-matter of the inquiry. Laotse himself spoke of it thus: "There is a thing which is all-containing, which was born before the existence of Heaven and Earth. How silent! How solitary! It stands alone and changes not. It revolves without danger to itself and is the mother of the universe. I do not know its name and so call it the Path. With reluctance I call it the Infinite. Infinity is the Fleeting, the Fleeting is the Vanishing, the Vanishing is the Reverting." The Tao is in the Passage rather than the Path. It is the spirit of Cosmic Change,—the eternal growth which returns upon itself to produce new forms. It recoils upon itself like the dragon, the beloved symbol of the Taoists. It folds and unfolds as do the clouds. The Tao might be spoken of as the Great Transition. Subjectively it is the Mood of the Universe. Its Absolute is the Relative.

It should be remembered in the first place that Taoism, like its legitimate successor, Zennism, represents the individualistic trend of the Southern Chinese mind in contra-distinction to the communism of Northern China which expressed itself in Confucianism. The Middle Kingdom is as vast as Europe and has a differentiation of idiosyncrasies marked by the two great river systems which traverse it. The Yangtse-Kiang and Hoang-Ho are respectively the Mediterranean and the Baltic. Even to-day, in spite of centuries of unification, the Southern Celestial differs in his thoughts and beliefs from his Northern brother as a member of the

Latin race differs from the Teuton. In ancient days, when communication was even more difficult than at present, and especially during the feudal period, this difference in thought was most pronounced. The art and poetry of the one breathes an atmosphere entirely distinct from that of the other. In Laotse and his followers and in Kutsugen, the forerunner of the Yangtse-Kiang naturepoets, we find an idealism quite inconsistent with the prosaic ethical notions of their contemporary northern writers. Laotse lived five centuries before the Christian Era.

The germ of Taoist speculation may be found long before the advent of Laotse, surnamed the Long-Eared. The archaic records of China, especially the Book of Changes, foreshadow his thought. But the great respect paid to the laws and customs of that classic period of Chinese civilisation which culminated with the establishment of the Chow dynasty in the twelfth century B.C., kept the development of individualism in check for a long while, so that it was not until after

the disintegration of the Chow dynasty and
the establishment of innumerable independent kingdoms that it was able to blossom
forth in the luxuriance of free-thought.
Laotse and Soshi (Chuangtse) were both
Southerners and the greatest exponents of the
New School. On the other hand Confucius
with his numerous disciples aimed at retain-
ing ancestral conventions. Taoism cannot be
understood without some knowledge of Confucianism and vice versa.

We have said that the Taoist Absolute
was the Relative. In ethics the Taoist railed
at the laws and the moral codes of society,
for to them right and wrong were but relative terms. Definition is always limitation—
the "fixed" and "unchangeless" are but
terms expressive of a stoppage of growth.
Said Kutsugen, "The Sages move the
world." Our standards of morality are be-
gotten of the past needs of society, but is
society to remain always the same? The observance of communal traditions involves a
constant sacrifice of the individual to the

state. Education, in order to keep up the mighty delusion, encourages a species of ignorance. People are not taught to be really virtuous, but to behave properly. We are wicked because we are frightfully self-conscious. We never forgive others because we know that we ourselves are in the wrong. We nurse a conscience because we are afraid to tell the truth to others; we take refuge in pride because we are afraid to tell the truth to ourselves. How can one be serious with the world when the world itself is so ridiculous! The spirit of barter is everywhere. Honour and Chastity! Behold the complacent salesman retailing the Good and True. One can even buy a so-called Religion, which is really but common morality sanctified with flowers and music. Rob the Church of her accessories and what remains behind? Yet the trusts thrive marvellously, for the prices are absurdly cheap,—a prayer for a ticket to heaven, a diploma for an honourable citizenship. Hide yourself under a bushel quickly, for if your real usefulness were

41

known to the world you would soon be knocked down to the highest bidder by the public auctioneer. Why do men and women like to advertise themselves so much? Is it not but an instinct derived from the days of slavery?

The virility of the idea lies not less in its power of breaking through contemporary thought than in its capacity for dominating subsequent movements. Taoism was an active power during the Shin dynasty, that epoch of Chinese unification from which we derive the name of China. It would be interesting had we time to note its influence on contemporary thinkers, the mathematicians, writers on law and war, the mystics and alchemists and the later nature-poets of the Yangtse-Kiang. We should not even ignore those speculators on Reality who doubted whether a white horse was real because he was white, or because he was solid, nor the Conversationalists of the Six dynasties who, like the Zen philosophers, revelled in discussions concerning the Pure and the Abstract.

Above all we should pay homage to Taoism
for what it has done toward the formation
of the Celestial character, giving to it a certain capacity for reserve and refinement as
"warm as jade." Chinese history is full of
instances in which the votaries of Taoism,
princes and hermits alike, followed with
varied and interesting results the teachings
of their creed. The tale will not be without
its quota of instruction and amusement. It
will be rich in anecdotes, allegories, and
aphorisms. We would fain be on speaking
terms with the delightful emperor who never
died because he never lived. We may ride
the wind with Liehtse and find it absolutely
quiet because we ourselves are the wind, or
dwell in mid-air with the Aged One of the
Hoang-Ho, who lived betwixt Heaven and
Earth because he was subject to neither the
one nor the other. Even in that grotesque
apology for Taoism which we find in China
at the present day, we can revel in a wealth
of imagery impossible to find in any other
cult.

But the chief contribution of Taoism to Asiatic life has been in the realm of aesthetics. Chinese historians have always spoken of Taoism as the "art of being in the world," for it deals with the present—ourselves. It is in us that God meets with Nature, and yesterday parts from to-morrow. The Present is the moving Infinity, the legitimate sphere of the Relative. Relativity seeks Adjustment; Adjustment is Art. The art of life lies in a constant readjustment to our surroundings. Taoism accepts the mundane as it is and, unlike the Confucians and the Buddhists, tries to find beauty in our world of woe and worry. The Sung allegory of the Three Vinegar Tasters explains admirably the trend of the three doctrines. Sakyamuni, Confucius, and Laotse once stood before a jar of vinegar—the emblem of life—and each dipped in his fingers to taste the brew. The matter-of-fact Confucius found it sour, the Buddha called it bitter, and Laotse pronounced it sweet.

The Taoists claimed that the comedy of

life could be made more interesting if everyone would preserve the unities. To keep the proportion of things and give place to others without losing one's own position was the secret of success in the mundane drama. We must know the whole play in order to properly act our parts; the conception of totality must never be lost in that of the individual. This Laotse illustrates by his favourite metaphor of the Vacuum. He claimed that only in vacuum lay the truly essential. The reality of a room, for instance, was to be found in the vacant space enclosed by the roof and walls, not in the roof and walls themselves. The usefulness of a water pitcher dwelt in the emptiness where water might be put, not in the form of the pitcher or the material of which it was made. Vacuum is all potent because all containing. In vacuum alone motion becomes possible. One who could make of himself a vacuum into which others might freely enter would become master of all situations. The whole can always dominate the part.

45

These Taoists' ideas have greatly influenced all our theories of action, even to those of fencing and wrestling. Jiu-jitsu, the Japanese art of self-defence, owes its name to a passage in the Taoteiking. In jiu-jitsu one seeks to draw out and exhaust the enemy's strength by non-resistance, vacuum, while conserving one's own strength for victory in the final struggle. In art the importance of the same principle is illustrated by the value of suggestion. In leaving something unsaid the beholder is given a chance to complete the idea and thus a great masterpiece irresistibly rivets your attention until you seem to become actually a part of it. A vacuum is there for you to enter and fill up to the full measure of your aesthetic emotion.

He who had made himself master of the art of living was the Real Man of the Taoist. At birth he enters the realm of dreams only to awaken to reality at death. He tempers his own brightness in order to merge himself into the obscurity of others. He is "reluctant, as one who crosses a stream in winter;

hesitating, as one who fears the neighbour-
hood; respectful, like a guest; trembling,
like ice that is about to melt; unassuming,
like a piece of wood not yet carved; vacant,
like a valley; formless, like troubled waters."
To him the three jewels of life were Pity,
Economy, and Modesty.

If now we turn our attention to Zennism
we shall find that it emphasises the teachings
of Taoism. Zen is a name derived from the
Sanscrit word Dhyana, which signifies meditation. It claims that through consecrated
meditation may be attained supreme self-
realisation. Meditation is one of the six ways
through which Buddhahood may be reached,
and the Zen sectarians affirm that Sakyamuni
laid special stress on this method in his later
teachings, handing down the rules to his
chief disciple Kashiapa. According to their
tradition Kashiapa, the first Zen patriarch,
imparted the secret to Ananda, who in turn
passed it on to successive patriarchs until it
reached Bodhi-Dharma, the twenty-eighth.
Bodhi-Dharma came to Northern China in

the early half of the sixth century and was
the first patriarch of Chinese Zen. There is
much uncertainty about the history of these
patriarchs and their doctrines. In its philosophical aspect early Zennism seems to have
affinity on one hand to the Indian Negativ-
ism of Nagarjuna and on the other to the
Gnan philosophy formulated by Sanchara-
charya. The first teaching of Zen as we know
it at the present day must be attributed to
the sixth Chinese patriarch Yeno (637–713),
founder of Southern Zen, so-called from the
fact of its predominance in Southern China.
He is closely followed by the great Baso
(died 788) who made of Zen a living influence in Celestial life. Hiakujo (719–814),
the pupil of Baso, first instituted the Zen
monastery and established a ritual and regula-
tions for its government. In the discussions
of the Zen school after the time of Baso we
find the play of the Yangtse-Kiang mind
causing an accession of native modes of
thought in contrast to the former Indian
idealism. Whatever sectarian pride may

assert to the contrary, one cannot help being impressed by the similarity of Southern Zen to the teachings of Laotse, and the Taoist Conversationalists. In the Taoteiking we already find allusions to the importance of self-concentration and the need of properly regulating the breath—essential points in the practice of Zen meditation. Some of the best commentaries on the Book of Laotse have been written by Zen scholars.

Zennism, like Taoism, is the worship of Relativity. One master defines Zen as the art of feeling the polar star in the southern sky. Truth can be reached only through the comprehension of opposites. Again, Zennism, like Taoism, is a strong advocate of individualism. Nothing is real except that which concerns the working of our own minds. Yeno, the sixth patriarch, once saw two monks watching the flag of a pagoda fluttering in the wind. One said "It is the wind that moves," the other said "It is the flag that moves"; but Yeno explained to them that the real movement was neither of the wind nor the flag, but of something within their own minds. Hiakujo was walking in the forest with a disciple when a hare scurried off at their approach. "Why does the hare fly from you?" asked Hiakujo. "Because he is afraid of me," was the answer. "No," said the master, "it is because you have a murderous instinct." This dialogue recalls that of Soshi (Chuangtse), the Taoist. One day Soshi was walking on the bank of a river with a friend. "How delightfully the fishes are enjoying themselves in the water!" exclaimed Soshi. His friend spake to him thus: "You are not a fish; how do you know that the fishes are enjoying themselves?" "You are not myself," returned Soshi; "how do you know that I do not know that the fishes are enjoying themselves?"

Zen was often opposed to the precepts of orthodox Buddhism even as Taoism was opposed to Confucianism. To the transcendental insight of the Zen, words were but an incumbrance to thought; the whole sway of Buddhist scriptures only commentaries on personal speculation. The followers of Zen aimed at direct communion with the inner nature of things, regarding their outward accessories only as impediments to a clear perception of Truth. It was this love of the Abstract that led the Zen to prefer black and white sketches to the elaborately coloured paintings of the classic Buddhist School. Some of the Zen even became iconoclastic as a result of their endeavour to recognise the Buddha in themselves rather than through images and symbolism. We find Tankawosho breaking up a wooden statue of Buddha on a wintry day to make a fire. "What sacrilege!" said the horror-stricken bystander. "I wish to get the Shali out of the ashes," calmly rejoined the Zen. "But you certainly will not get Shali from this image!" was the angry retort, to which Tanka replied, "If I do not, this is certainly not a Buddha and I am committing no sacrilege." Then he turned to warm himself over the kindling fire.

A special contribution of Zen to Eastern thought was its recognition of the mundane as of equal importance with the spiritual. It held that in the great relation of things there was no distinction of small and great, an atom possessing equal possibilities with the universe. The seeker for perfection must discover in his own life the reflection of the inner light. The organisation of the Zen monastery was very significant of this point of view. To every member, except the abbot, was assigned some special work in the care-taking of the monastery, and curiously enough, to the novices were committed the lighter duties, while to the most respected and advanced monks were given the more irksome and menial tasks. Such services formed a part of the Zen discipline and every least action must be done absolutely perfectly. Thus many a weighty discussion ensued while weeding the garden, paring a turnip, or serving tea. The whole ideal of Teaism is a result of this Zen conception of greatness in the smallest incidents of life. Taoism furnished the basis for aesthetic ideals, Zen-nism made them practical.

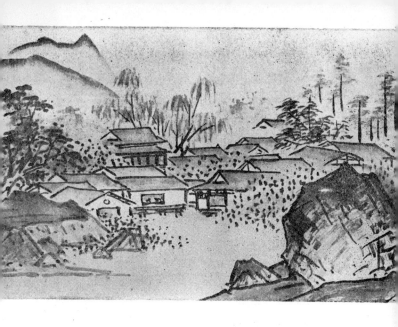

THE TEA-ROOM

To EUROPEAN architects brought up on the traditions of stone and brick construction, our Japanese method of building with wood and bamboo seems scarcely worthy to be ranked as architecture. It is but quite recently that a competent student of Western architecture has recognised and paid tribute to the remarkable perfection of our great temples. Such being the case as regards our classic architecture, we could hardly expect the outsider to appreciate the subtle beauty of the tea-room, its principles of construction and decoration being entirely different from those of the West.

The tea-room (the Sukiya) does not pretend to be other than a mere cottage—a straw hut, as we call it. The original ideographs for Sukiya mean the Abode of Fancy. Latterly the various tea-masters substituted various Chinese characters according to their conception of the tea-room, and the term Sukiya may signify the Abode of Vacancy or the Abode of the Unsymmetrical. It is an Abode of Fancy inasmuch as it is an ephemeral structure built to house a poetic impulse. It is an Abode of Vacancy inasmuch as it is devoid of ornamentation except for what may be placed in it to satisfy some aesthetic need of the moment. It is an Abode of the Unsymmetrical inasmuch as it is consecrated to the worship of the Imperfect, purposely leaving some thing unfinished for the play of the imagination to complete. The ideals of Teaism have since the sixteenth century influenced our architecture to such a degree that the ordinary Japanese interior of the present day, on account of the extreme simplicity and chasteness of its scheme of decoration, appears to foreigners almost barren.

The first independent tea-room was the creation of Senno-Soyeki, commonly known by his later name of Rikiu, the greatest of all tea-masters, who, in the sixteenth century, under the patronage of Taiko-Hideyoshi, instituted and brought to a high state of perfection the formalities of the Tea-ceremony. The proportions of the tea-room had been previously determined by Jowo—a famous tea-master of the fifteenth century. The early tea-room consisted merely of a portion of the ordinary drawing-room partitioned off by screens for the purpose of the tea-gathering. The portion partitioned off was called the Kakoi (enclosure), a name still applied to those tea-rooms which are built into a house and are not independent constructions. The Sukiya consists of the tea-room proper, designed to accommodate not more than five persons, a number suggestive of the saying "more than the Graces and less than the Muses," an anteroom (midsuya) where the tea utensils are washed and arranged before being brought in, a portico (machiai) in which the guests wait until they receive the summons to enter the tea-room, and a garden path (the roji) which connects the machiai with the tea-room. The tea-room is unimpressive in appearance. It is smaller than the smallest of Japanese houses, while the materials used in its construction are intended to give the suggestion of refined poverty. Yet we must remember that all this is the result of profound artistic forethought, and that the details have been worked out with care perhaps even greater than that expended on the building of the richest palaces and temples. A good tea-room is more costly than an ordinary mansion, for the selection of its materials, as well as its workmanship, re-

quires immense care and precision. Indeed the
carpenters employed by the tea-masters form
a distinct and highly honoured class among
artisans, their work being no less delicate
than that of the makers of lacquer cabinets.

The tea-room is not only different from
any production of Western architecture, but
also contrasts strongly with the classical
architecture of Japan itself. Our ancient noble
edifices, whether secular or ecclesiastical, were
not to be despised even as regards their mere
size. The few that have been spared in the
disastrous conflagrations of centuries are still
capable of aweing us by the grandeur and
richness of their decoration. Huge pillars of
wood from two to three feet in diameter and
from thirty to forty feet high, supported, by
a complicated network of brackets, the
enormous beams which groaned under the
weight of the tile-covered slanting roofs. The
material and mode of construction, though
weak against fire, proved itself strong against
earthquakes, and was well suited to the
climatic conditions of the country. In the

Golden Hall of Horiuji and the Pagoda of Yakushiji, we have noteworthy examples of the durability of our wooden architecture. These buildings have practically stood intact for nearly twelve centuries. The interior of the old temples and palaces was profusely decorated. In the Hoōdo temple at Uji, dating from the tenth century, we can still see the elaborate canopy and gilded baldachinos, many-coloured and inlaid with mirrors and mother-of-pearl, as well as remains of the paintings and sculpture which formerly covered the walls. Later, at Nikko and in the Nijo castle in Kyoto, we see structural beauty sacrificed to a wealth of ornamentation which in colour and exquisite detail equals the utmost gorgeousness of Arabian or Moorish effort.

The simplicity and purism of the tea-room resulted from emulation of the Zen monastery. A Zen monastery differs from those of other Buddhist sects inasmuch as it is meant only to be a dwelling place for the monks. Its chapel is not a place of worship or pil-

grimage, but a college room where the students congregate for discussion and the practice of meditation. The room is bare except
for a central alcove in which, behind the
altar, is a statue of Bodhi Dharma, the
founder of the sect, or of Sakyamuni attended
by Kashiapa and Ananda, the two earliest
Zen patriarchs. On the altar, flowers and incense are offered up in memory of the great
contributions which these sages made to Zen.
We have already said that it was the ritual
instituted by the Zen monks of successively
drinking tea out of a bowl before the image
of Bodhi Dharma, which laid the foundations
of the tea-ceremony. We might add here that
the altar of the Zen chapel was the prototype
of the Tokonoma,—the place of honour in a
Japanese room where paintings and flowers
are placed for the edification of the guests.

All our great tea-masters were students of
Zen and attempted to introduce the spirit of
Zennism into the actualities of life. Thus the
room, like the other equipments of the tea-
ceremony, reflects many of the Zen doctrines.

The size of the orthodox tea-room, which is
four mats and a half, or ten feet square, is
determined by a passage in the Sutra of
Vikramadytia. In that interesting work,
Vikramadytia welcomes the Saint Manjushiri
and eighty-four thousand disciples of Buddha
in a room of this size,—an allegory based on
the theory of the non-existence of space to
the truly enlightened. Again the roji, the
garden path which leads from the machiai
to the tea-room, signified the first stage of
meditation,—the passage into self-illumina-
tion. The roji was intended to break connection with the outside world, and to produce
a fresh sensation conducive to the full enjoyment of aestheticism in the tea-room itself.
One who has trodden this garden path cannot fail to remember how his spirit, as he
walked in the twilight of evergreens over the
regular irregularities of the stepping stones,
beneath which lay dried pine needles, and
passed beside the moss-covered granite
lanterns, became uplifted above ordinary
thoughts. One may be in the midst of a city,

and yet feel as if he were in the forest far away from the dust and din of civilisation. Great was the ingenuity displayed by the tea-masters in producing these effects of serenity and purity. The nature of the sensations to be aroused in passing through the roji differed with different tea-masters. Some, like Rikiu, aimed at utter loneliness, and claimed the secret of making a roji was contained in the ancient ditty:

"I looked beyond;
Flowers are not,
Nor tinted leaves.
On the sea beach
A solitary cottage stands
In the waning light
Of an autumn eve."

Others, like Kobori-Enshiu, sought for a different effect. Enshiu said the idea of the garden path was to be found in the following verses:

"A cluster of summer trees,
A bit of the sea,
A pale evening moon."

It is not difficult to gather his meaning. He wished to create the attitude of a newly-awakened soul still lingering amid shadowy dreams of the past, yet bathing in the sweet unconsciousness of a mellow spiritual light, and yearning for the freedom that lay in the expanse beyond.

Thus prepared the guest will silently approach the sanctuary, and, if a samurai, will leave his sword on the rack beneath the eaves, the tea-room being preëminently the house of peace. Then he will bend low and creep into the room through a small door not more than three feet in height. This proceeding was incumbent on all guests,—high and low alike,—and was intended to inculcate humility. The order of precedence having been mutually agreed upon while resting in the machiai, the guests one by one will enter noiselessly and take their seats, first making obeisance to the picture or flower arrangement on the tokonoma. The host will not enter the room until all the guests have seated themselves and quiet reigns with nothing to break the silence save the note of the boiling water in the iron kettle. The kettle sings well, for pieces of iron are so arranged in the bottom as to produce a peculiar melody in which one may hear the echoes of a cataract muffled by clouds, of a distant sea breaking among the rocks, a rainstorm sweeping through a bamboo forest, or of the soughing of pines on some faraway hill.

Even in the daytime the light in the room is subdued, for the low eaves of the slanting roof admit but few of the sun's rays. Everything is sober in tint from the ceiling to the floor; the guests themselves have carefully chosen garments of unobtrusive colours. The mellowness of age is over all, everything suggestive of recent acquirement being tabooed save only the one note of contrast furnished by the bamboo dipper and the linen napkin, both immaculately white and new. However faded the tea-room and the tea-equipage may seem, everything is absolutely clean. Not a particle of dust will be found in the darkest corner, for if any exists the host is not a tea-

master. One of the first requisites of a tea-
master is the knowledge of how to sweep,
clean, and wash, for there is an art in clean-
ing and dusting. A piece of antique metal
work must not be attacked with the un-
scrupulous zeal of the Dutch housewife.
Dripping water from a flower vase need not
be wiped away, for it may be suggestive of
dew and coolness.

In this connection there is a story of Rikiu
which well illustrates the ideas of cleanliness
entertained by the tea-masters. Rikiu was
watching his son Shoan as he swept and
watered the garden path. "Not clean enough,"
said Rikiu, when Shoan had finished his
task, and bade him try again. After a weary
hour the son turned to Rikiu: "Father, there
is nothing more to be done. The steps have
been washed for the third time, the stone
lanterns and the trees are well sprinkled with
water, moss and lichens are shining with a
fresh verdure; not a twig, not a leaf have I
left on the ground." "Young fool," chided
the tea-master, "that is not the way a garden

path should be swept." Saying this, Rikiu stepped into the garden, shook a tree and scattered over the garden gold and crimson leaves, scraps of the brocade of autumn! What Rikiu demanded was not cleanliness alone, but the beautiful and the natural also.

The name, Abode of Fancy, implies a structure created to meet some individual artistic requirement. The tea-room is made for the tea-master not the tea-master for the tea-room. It is not intended for posterity and is therefore ephemeral. The idea that everyone should have a house of his own is based on an ancient custom of the Japanese race, Shinto superstition ordaining that every dwelling should be evacuated on the death of its chief occupant. Perhaps there may have been some unrealised sanitary reason for this practice. Another early custom was that a newly built house should be provided for each couple that married. It is on account of such customs that we find the Imperial capitals so frequently removed from one site to another in ancient days. The rebuilding, every twenty years, of Ise Temple, the supreme shrine of the Sun-Goddess, is an example of one of these ancient rites which still obtain at the present day. The observance of these customs was only possible with some such form of construction as that furnished by our system of wooden architecture, easily pulled down, easily built up. A more lasting style, employing brick and stone, would have rendered migrations impracticable, as indeed they became when the more stable and massive wooden construction of China was adopted by us after the Nara period.

With the predominance of Zen individualism in the fifteenth century, however, the old idea became imbued with a deeper significance as conceived in connection with the tea-room. Zennism, with the Buddhist theory of evanescence and its demands for the mastery of spirit over matter, recognised the house only as a temporary refuge for the body. The body itself was but as a hut in the wilderness, a flimsy shelter made by tying together the grasses that grew around,—when these ceased to be bound together they again became resolved into the original waste. In the tea-room fugitiveness is suggested in the thatched roof, frailty in the slender pillars, lightness in the bamboo support, apparent carelessness in the use of commonplace materials. The eternal is to be found only in the spirit which, embodied in these simple surroundings, beautifies them with the subtle light of its refinement.

That the tea-room should be built to suit some individual taste is an enforcement of the principle of vitality in art. Art, to be fully appreciated, must be true to contemporaneous life. It is not that we should ignore the claims of posterity, but that we should seek to enjoy the present more. It is not that we should disregard the creations of the past, but that we should try to assimilate them into our consciousness. Slavish conformity to traditions and formulas fetters the expression of individuality in architecture. We can but weep over those senseless imitations of European buildings which one beholds in modern Japan. We marvel why, among the most progressive Western nations, architecture should be so devoid of originality, so replete with repetitions of obsolete styles. Perhaps we are now passing through an age of democratisation in art, while awaiting the rise of some princely master who shall establish a new dynasty. Would that we loved the ancients more and copied them less! It has been said that the Greeks were great because they never drew from the antique.

The term, Abode of Vacancy, besides conveying the Taoist theory of the all-containing, involves the conception of a continued need of change in decorative motives. The tea-room is absolutely empty, except for what may be placed there temporarily to satisfy some aesthetic mood. Some special art object is brought in for the occasion, and everything else is selected and arranged to enhance the beauty of the principal theme. One cannot listen to different pieces of music at the same time, a real comprehension of the beautiful being possible only through concentration upon some central motive. Thus it will be seen that the system of decoration in our tea-rooms is opposed to that which obtains in the West, where the interior of a house is often converted into a museum. To a Japanese, accustomed to simplicity of ornamentation and frequent change of decorative method, a Western interior permanently filled with a vast array of pictures, statuary, and bric-à-brac gives the impression of mere vulgar display of riches. It calls for a mighty wealth of appreciation to enjoy the constant sight of even a masterpiece, and limitless indeed must be the capacity for artistic feeling in those who can exist day after day in the midst of such confusion of colour and form as is to be often seen in the homes of Europe and America.

The "Abode of the Unsymmetrical" suggests another phase of our decorative scheme. The absence of symmetry in Japanese art objects has been often commented on by Western critics. This, also, is a result of a working out through Zennism of Taoist ideals. Confucianism, with its deep-seated idea of dualism, and Northern Buddhism with its worship of a trinity, were in no way opposed to the expression of symmetry. As a matter of fact, if we study the ancient bronzes of China or the religious arts of the Tang dynasty and the Nara period, we shall recognise a constant striving after symmetry. The decoration of our classical interiors was decidedly regular in its arrangement. The Taoist and Zen conception of perfection, however, was different. The dynamic nature of their philosophy laid more stress upon the process through which perfection was sought than upon perfection itself. True beauty could be discovered only by one who mentally completed the incomplete. The virility of life and art lay in its possibilities for growth. In the tea-room it is left for each guest in imagination to complete the total effect in relation to himself. Since Zennism has become the prevailing mode of thought, the art of the extreme Orient has purposely avoided the symmetrical as expressing not only completion, but repetition. Uniformity of design was considered as fatal to the freshness of imagination. Thus, landscapes, birds, and flowers became the favourite subjects for depiction rather than the human figure, the latter being present in the person of the beholder himself. We are often too much in evidence as it is, and in spite of our vanity even self-regard is apt to become monotonous.

In the tea-room the fear of repetition is a constant presence. The various objects for the decoration of a room should be so selected that no colour or design shall be repeated. If you have a living flower, a painting of flowers is not allowable. If you are using a round kettle, the water pitcher should be angular. A cup with a black glaze should not be associated with a tea-caddy of black lacquer. In placing a vase or an incense burner on the tokonoma, care should be taken not to put it in the exact centre, lest it divide the space into equal halves. The pillar of the tokonoma should be of a different kind of wood from

71

the other pillars, in order to break any suggestion of monotony in the room.

Here again the Japanese method of interior decoration differs from that of the Occident, where we see objects arrayed symmetrically on mantelpieces and elsewhere. In Western houses we are often confronted with what appears to us useless reiteration. We find it trying to talk to a man while his full-length portrait stares at us from behind his back. We wonder which is real, he of the picture or he who talks, and feel a curious conviction that one of them must be fraud. Many a time have we sat at a festive board contemplating, with a secret shock to our digestion, the representation of abundance on the dining-room walls. Why these pictured victims of chase and sport, the elaborate carvings of fishes and fruit? Why the display of family plates, reminding us of those who have dined and are dead?

The simplicity of the tea-room and its freedom from vulgarity make it truly a sanctuary from the vexations of the outer

72

world. There and there alone can one consecrate himself to undisturbed adoration of the beautiful. In the sixteenth century the tearoom afforded a welcome respite from labour to the fierce warriors and statesmen engaged in the unification and reconstruction of Japan. In the seventeenth century, after the strict formalism of the Tokugawa rule had been developed, it offered the only opportunity possible for the free communion of artistic spirits. Before a great work of art there was no distinction between daimyo, samurai, and commoner. Nowadays industrialism is making true refinement more and more difficult all the world over. Do we not need the tearoom more than ever?

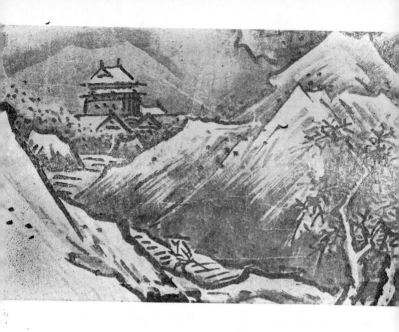

ART APPRECIATION

Have you heard the Taoist tale of the Taming of the Harp?

Once in the hoary ages in the Ravine of Lungmen stood a Kiri tree, a veritable king of the forest. It reared its head to talk to the stars; its roots struck deep into the earth, mingling their bronzed coils with those of the silver dragon that slept beneath. And it came

to pass that a mighty wizard made of this
tree a wondrous harp, whose stubborn spirit
should be tamed but by the greatest of musicians. For long the instrument was treasured
by the Emperor of China, but all in vain
were the efforts of those who in turn tried
to draw melody from its strings. In response
to their utmost strivings there came from the
harp but harsh notes of disdain, ill-according
with the songs they fain would sing. The
harp refused to recognise a master.

At last came Peiwoh, the prince of harp-
ists. With tender hand he caressed the harp as
one might seek to soothe an unruly horse,
and softly touched the chords. He sang of
nature and the seasons, of high mountains
and flowing waters, and all the memories
of the tree awoke! Once more the sweet
breath of spring played amidst its branches.
The young cataracts, as they danced down
the ravine, laughed to the budding flowers.
Anon were heard the dreamy voices of summer with its myriad insects, the gentle patter-
ing of rain, the wail of the cuckoo. Hark! a

tiger roars,—the valley answers again. It is autumn; in the desert night, sharp like a sword gleams the moon upon the frosted grass. Now winter reigns, and through the snow-filled air swirl flocks of swans and rattling hailstones beat upon the boughs with fierce delight.

Then Peiwoh changed the key and sang of love. The forest swayed like an ardent swain deep lost in thought. On high, like a haughty maiden, swept a cloud bright and fair; but passing, trailed long shadows on the ground, black like despair. Again the mode was changed; Peiwoh sang of war, of clashing steel and trampling steeds. And in the harp arose the tempest of Lungmen, the dragon rode the lightning, the thundering avalanche crashed through the hills. In ecstacy the Celestial monarch asked Peiwoh wherein lay the secret of his victory. "Sire," he replied, "others have failed because they sang but of themselves. I left the harp to choose its theme, and knew not truly whether the harp had been Peiwoh or Peiwoh were the harp."

This story well illustrates the mystery of art appreciation. The masterpiece is a symphony played upon our finest feelings. True art is Peiwoh, and we the harp of Lungmen. At the magic touch of the beautiful the secret chords of our being are awakened, we vibrate and thrill in response to its call. Mind speaks to mind. We listen to the unspoken, we gaze upon the unseen. The master calls forth notes we know not of. Memories long forgotten all come back to us with a new significance. Hopes stifled by fear, yearnings that we dare not recognise, stand forth in new glory. Our mind is the canvas on which the artists lay their colour; their pigments are our emotions; their chiaroscuro the light of joy, the shadow of sadness. The masterpiece is of ourselves, as we are of the masterpiece.

The sympathetic communion of minds necessary for art appreciation must be based on mutual concession. The spectator must cultivate the proper attitude for receiving the message, as the artist must know to impart it. The tea-master, Kobori-Enshiu, himself a daimyo, has left to us these memorable words: "Approach a great painting as thou wouldst approach a great prince." In order to understand a masterpiece, you must lay yourself low before it and await with bated breath its least utterance. An eminent Sung critic once made a charming confession. Said he: "In my young days I praised the master whose pictures I liked, but as my judgment matured I praised myself for liking what the masters had chosen to have me like." It is to be deplored that so few of us really take pains to study the moods of the masters. In our stubborn ignorance we refuse to render them this simple courtesy, and thus often miss the rich repast of beauty spread before our very eyes. A master has always something to offer, while we go hungry solely because of our own lack of appreciation.

To the sympathetic a masterpiece becomes a living reality towards which we feel drawn in bonds of comradeship. The masters are immortal, for their loves and fears live in us over and over again. It is rather the soul than

the hand, the man than the technique, which
appeals to us,—the more human the call the
deeper is our response. It is because of this
secret understanding between the master and
ourselves that in poetry or romance we suffer
and rejoice with the hero and heroine. Chikamatsu, our Japanese Shakespeare, has laid
down as one of the first principles of dramatic composition the importance of taking the
audience into the confidence of the author.
Several of his pupils submitted plays for his
approval, but only one of the pieces appealed
to him. It was a play somewhat resembling
the Comedy of Errors, in which twin
brethren suffer through mistaken identity.
"This," said Chikamatsu, "has the proper
spirit of the drama, for it takes the audience
into consideration. The public is permitted
to know more than the actors. It knows where
the mistake lies, and pities the poor figures
on the board who innocently rush to their
fate."

The great masters both of the East and the
West never forgot the value of suggestion as

a means for taking the spectator into their
confidence. Who can contemplate a masterpiece without being awed by the immense
vista of thought presented to our consideration? How familiar and sympathetic are they
all; how cold in contrast the modern com-
monplaces! In the former we feel the warm
outpouring of a man's heart; in the latter
only a formal salute. Engrossed in his technique, the modern rarely rises above himself.
Like the musicians who vainly invoked the
Lungmen harp, he sings only of himself. His
works may be nearer science, but are further
from humanity. We have an old saying in
Japan that a woman cannot love a man who
is truly vain, for there is no crevice in his
heart for love to enter and fill up. In art
vanity is equally fatal to sympathetic feeling,
whether on the part of the artist or the public.

Nothing is more hallowing than the union
of kindred spirits in art. At the moment of
meeting, the art lover transcends himself. At
once he is and is not. He catches a glimpse
of Infinity, but words cannot voice his de-

light, for the eye has no tongue. Freed from the fetters of matter, his spirit moves in the rhythm of things. It is thus that art becomes akin to religion and ennobles mankind. It is this which makes a masterpiece something sacred. In the old days the veneration in which the Japanese held the work of the great artist was intense. The tea-masters guarded their treasures with religious secrecy, and it was often necessary to open a whole series of boxes, one within another, before reaching the shrine itself—the silken wrapping within whose soft folds lay the holy of holies. Rarely was the object exposed to view, and then only to the initiated.

At the time when Teaism was in the ascendency the Taiko's generals would be better satisfied with the present of a rare work of art than a large grant of territory as a reward of victory. Many of our favourite dramas are based on the loss and recovery of a noted masterpiece. For instance, in one play the palace of Lord Hosokawa, in which was preserved the celebrated painting of Dharuma by

Sesson, suddenly takes fire through the negli-
gence of the samurai in charge. Resolved at
all hazards to rescue the precious painting,
he rushes into the burning building and seizes
the kakemono, only to find all means of exit
cut off by the flames. Thinking only of the
picture, he slashes open his body with his
sword, wraps his torn sleeve about the Sesson, and plunges it into the gaping wound.
The fire is at last extinguished. Among the
smoking embers is found a half-consumed
corpse, within which reposes the treasure un-
injured by the fire. Horrible as such tales are,
they illustrate the great value that we set upon
a masterpiece, as well as the devotion of a
trusted samurai.

We must remember, however, that art is
of value only to the extent that it speaks to
us. It might be a universal language if we
ourselves were universal in our sympathies.
Our finite nature, the power of tradition and
conventionality, as well as our hereditary in-
stincts, restrict the scope of our capacity for
artistic enjoyment. Our very individuality

establishes in one sense a limit to our understanding; and our aesthetic personality seeks
its own affinities in the creations of the past.
It is true that with cultivation our sense of
art appreciation broadens, and we become
able to enjoy many hitherto unrecognised
expressions of beauty. But, after all, we see
only our own image in the universe,—our
particular idiosyncrasies dictate the mode of
our perceptions. The tea-masters collected only
objects which fell strictly within the measure
of their individual appreciation.

One is reminded in this connection of a
story concerning Kobori-Enshiu. Enshiu was
complimented by his disciples on the admir-
able taste he had displayed in the choice of
his collection. Said they, "Each piece is such
that no one could help admiring. It shows
that you had better taste than had Rikiu, for
his collection could only be appreciated by
one beholder in a thousand." Sorrowfully
Enshiu replied: "This only proves how commonplace I am. The great Rikiu dared to
love only those objects which personally ap-

pealed to him, whereas I unconsciously cater to the taste of the majority. Verily, Rikiu was one in a thousand among tea-masters."

It is much to be regretted that so much of the apparent enthusiasm for art at the present day has no foundation in real feeling. In this democratic age of ours men clamour for what is popularly considered the best, regardless of their feelings. They want the costly, not the refined; the fashionable, not the beautiful. To the masses, contemplation of illustrated periodicals, the worthy product of their own industrialism, would give more digestible food for artistic enjoyment than the early Italians or the Ashikaga masters, whom they pretend to admire. The name of the artist is more important to them than the quality of the work. As a Chinese critic complained many centuries ago, "People criticise a picture by their ear." It is this lack of genuine appreciation that is responsible for the pseudo-classic horrors that to-day greet us wherever we turn.

Another common mistake is that of con-

fusing art with archaeology. The veneration
born of antiquity is one of the best traits in
the human character, and fain would we
have it cultivated to a greater extent. The old
masters are rightly to be honoured for open-
ing the path to future enlightenment. The
mere fact that they have passed unscathed
through centuries of criticism and come down
to us still covered with glory commands our
respect. But we should be foolish indeed if
we valued their achievement simply on the
score of age. Yet we allow our historical sympathy to override our aesthetic discrimina-
tion. We offer flowers of approbation when
the artist is safely laid in his grave. The
nineteenth century, pregnant with the theory
of evolution, has moreover created in us
the habit of losing sight of the individual in
the species. A collector is anxious to acquire
specimens to illustrate a period or a school,
and forgets that a single masterpiece can teach
us more than any number of the mediocre
products of a given period or school. We classify too much and enjoy too little. The sacri-

fice of the aesthetic to the so-called scientific method of exhibition has been the bane of many museums.

The claims of contemporary art cannot be ignored in any vital scheme of life. The art of to-day is that which really belongs to us: it is our own reflection. In condemning it we but condemn ourselves. We say that the present age possesses no art:—who is responsible for this? It is indeed a shame that despite all our rhapsodies about the ancients we pay so little attention to our own possibilities. Struggling artists, weary souls lingering in the shadow of cold disdain! In our self-centred century, what inspiration do we offer them? The past may well look with pity at the poverty of our civilisation; the future will laugh at the barrenness of our art. We are destroying art in destroying the beautiful in life. Would that some great wizard might from the stem of society shape a mighty harp whose strings would resound to the touch of genius.

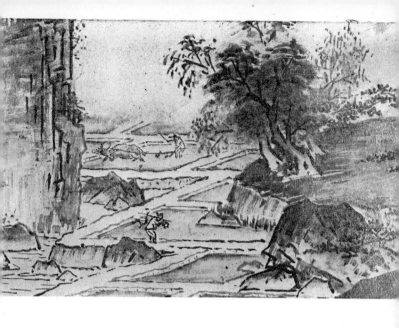

FLOWERS

IN THE trembling grey of a spring dawn, when the birds were whispering in mysterious cadence among the trees, have you not felt that they were talking to their mates about the flowers? Surely with mankind the appreciation of flowers must have been coeval with the poetry of love. Where better than in a flower, sweet in its unconsciousness, fragrant because of its silence, can we image the unfolding of a virgin soul? The primeval man in offering the first garland to his maiden thereby transcended the brute. He became human in thus rising above the crude necessities of nature. He entered the realm of art when he perceived the subtle use of the useless.

In joy or sadness, flowers are our constant friends. We eat, drink, sing, dance, and flirt with them. We wed and christen with flowers. We dare not die without them. We have worshipped with the lily, we have meditated with the lotus, we have charged in battle array with the rose and the chrysanthemum. We have even attempted to speak in the language of flowers. How could we live without them? It frightens one to conceive of a world bereft of their presence. What solace do they not bring to the bedside of the sick, what a light of bliss to the darkness of weary spirits? Their serene tenderness restores to us our waning confidence in the universe even as the intent gaze of a beautiful child recalls our lost hopes. When we are laid low in the dust it is they who linger in sorrow over our graves.

Sad as it is, we cannot conceal the fact that in spite of our companionship with flowers we have not risen very far above the brute. Scratch the sheepskin and the wolf within us will soon show his teeth. It has been said that man at ten is an animal, at twenty a lunatic, at thirty a failure, at forty a fraud, and at fifty a criminal. Perhaps he becomes a criminal because he has never ceased to be an animal. Nothing is real to us but hunger, nothing sacred except our own desires. Shrine after shrine has crumbled before our eyes; but one altar forever is preserved, that whereon we burn incense to the supreme idol, —ourselves. Our god is great, and money is his Prophet! We devastate nature in order to make sacrifice to him. We boast that we have conquered Matter and forget that it is Matter that has enslaved us. What atrocities do we not perpetrate in the name of culture and refinement!

Tell me, gentle flowers, teardrops of the stars, standing in the garden, nodding your heads to the bees as they sing of the dews and the sunbeams, are you aware of the fearful doom that awaits you? Dream on, sway and frolic while you may in the gentle breezes of summer. To-morrow a ruthless hand will close around your throats. You will be wrenched, torn asunder limb by limb, and borne away from your quiet homes. The wretch, she may be passing fair. She may say how lovely you are while her fingers are still moist with your blood. Tell me, will this be kindness? It may be your fate to be imprisoned in the hair of one whom you know to be heartless or to be thrust into the buttonhole of one who would not dare to look you in the face were you a man. It may even be your lot to be confined in some narrow vessel with only stagnant water to quench the maddening thirst that warns of ebbing life.

Flowers, if you were in the land of the Mikado, you might some time meet a dread personage armed with scissors and a tiny saw.

He would call himself a Master of Flowers.
He would claim the rights of a doctor and
you would instinctively hate him, for you
know a doctor always seeks to prolong the
troubles of his victims. He would cut, bend,
and twist you into those impossible positions
which he thinks it proper that you should
assume. He would contort your muscles and
dislocate your bones like any osteopath. He
would burn you with red-hot coals to stop
your bleeding, and thrust wires into you to
assist your circulation. He would diet you
with salt, vinegar, alum, and sometimes,
vitriol. Boiling water would be poured on
your feet when you seemed ready to faint.
It would be his boast that he could keep life
within you for two or more weeks longer
than would have been possible without his
treatment. Would you not have preferred to
have been killed at once when you were first
captured? What were the crimes you must
have committed during your past incarna-
tion to warrant such punishment as this?

The wanton waste of flowers among Western communities is even more appalling than the way they are treated by Eastern Flower-Masters. The number of flowers cut daily to adorn the ballrooms and banquet-tables of Europe and America, to be thrown away on the morrow, must be something enormous; if strung together they might garland a continent. Beside this utter carelessness of life, the guilt of the Flower-Master becomes insignificant. He, at least, respects the economy of nature, selects his victims with careful foresight, and after death does honour to their remains. In the West the display of flowers seems to be a part of the pageantry of wealth,—the fancy of a moment. Whither do they all go, these flowers, when the revelry is over? Nothing is more pitiful than to see a faded flower remorselessly flung upon a dung heap.

Why were the flowers born so beautiful and yet so hapless? Insects can sting, and even the meekest of beasts will fight when brought to bay. The bird whose plumage is sought to deck some bonnet can fly from its pursuer, the furred animal whose coat you covet for your own may hide at your approach. Alas! The only flower known to have wings is the butterfly; all others stand helpless before the destroyer. If they shriek in their death agony their cry never reaches our hardened ears. We are ever brutal to those who love and serve us in silence, but the time may come when, for our cruelty, we shall be deserted by these best friends of ours. Have you not noticed that the wild flowers are becoming scarcer every year? It may be that their wise men have told them to depart till man becomes more human. Perhaps they have migrated to heaven.

Much may be said in favour of him who cultivates plants. The man of the pot is far more humane than he of the scissors. We watch with delight his concern about water and sunshine, his feuds with parasites, his horror of frosts, his anxiety when the buds come slowly, his rapture when the leaves attain their lustre. In the East the art of floriculture is a very ancient one, and the loves of a poet and his favourite plant have often been recorded in story and song. With the development of ceramics during the Tang and Sung dynasties we hear of wonderful receptacles made to hold plants, not pots, but jewelled palaces. A special attendant was detailed to wait upon each flower and to wash its leaves with soft brushes made of rabbit hair. It has been written that the peony should be bathed by a handsome maiden in full costume, that a winter-plum should be watered by a pale, slender monk. In Japan, one of the most popular of the No-dances, the Hachi-noki, composed during the Ashikaga period, is based upon the story of an impoverished knight, who, on a freezing night, in lack of fuel for a fire, cuts his cherished plants in order to entertain a wandering friar. The friar is in reality no other than Hojo-Toki-yori, the Haroun-Al-Raschid of our tales, and the sacrifice is not without its reward. This opera never fails to draw tears from a Tokio audience even to-day.

Great precautions were taken for the pre-

servation of delicate blossoms. Emperor
Huensung, of the Tang dynasty, hung tiny
golden bells on the branches in his garden to
keep off the birds. He it was who went off
in the springtime with his court musicians
to gladden the flowers with soft music. A
quaint tablet, which tradition ascribes to
Yoshitsune, the hero of our Arthurian legends, is still extant in one of the Japanese
monasteries. It is a notice put up for the
protection of a certain wonderful plum-tree,
and appeals to us with the grim humour of
a warlike age. After referring to the beauty
of the blossoms, the inscription says: "Who-
ever cuts a single branch of this tree shall
forfeit a finger therefor." Would that such
laws could be enforced nowadays against
those who wantonly destroy flowers and
mutilate objects of art!

Yet even in the case of pot flowers we are
inclined to suspect the selfishness of man.
Why take the plants from their homes and
ask them to bloom mid strange surroundings?
Is it not like asking the birds to sing and

mate cooped up in cages? Who knows but that the orchids feel stifled by the artificial heat in your conservatories and hopelessly long for a glimpse of their own Southern skies?

The ideal lover of flowers is he who visits them in their native haunts, like Taoyuen-ming, who sat before a broken bamboo fence in converse with the wild chrysanthemum, or Linwosing, losing himself amid mysterious fragrance as he wandered in the twilight among the plum-blossoms of the Western Lake. 'Tis said that Chowmushih slept in a boat so that his dreams might mingle with those of the lotus. It was this same spirit which moved the Empress Komio, one of our most renowned Nara sovereigns, as she sang: "If I pluck thee, my hand will defile thee, O Flower! Standing in the meadows as thou art, I offer thee to the Buddhas of the past, of the present, of the future."

However, let us not be too sentimental. Let us be less luxurious but more magnificent. Said Laotse: "Heaven and earth are pitiless."

Said Kobodaishi: "Flow, flow, flow, flow, the current of life is ever onward. Die, die, die, die, death comes to all." Destruction faces us wherever we turn. Destruction below and above, destruction behind and before. Change is the only Eternal,—why not as welcome Death as Life? They are but counterparts one of the other,—the Night and Day of Brahma. Through the disintegration of the old, re-creation becomes possible. We have worshipped Death, the relentless goddess of mercy, under many different names. It was the shadow of the All-devouring that the Gheburs greeted in the fire. It is the icy purism of the sword-soul before which Shinto-Japan prostrates herself even to-day. The mystic fire consumes our weakness, the sacred sword cleaves the bondage of desire. From our ashes springs the phoenix of celestial hope, out of the freedom comes a higher realisation of manhood.

Why not destroy flowers if thereby we can evolve new forms ennobling the world idea? We only ask them to join in our sacrifice to

the beautiful. We shall atone for the deed
by consecrating ourselves to Purity and Simplicity. Thus reasoned the tea-masters when
they established the Cult of Flowers.

Anyone acquainted with the ways of our
tea- and flower-masters must have noticed the
religious veneration with which they regard
flowers. They do not cull at random, but
carefully select each branch or spray with an
eye to the artstic composition they have in
mind. They would be ashamed should they
chance to cut more than were absolutely
necessary. It may be remarked in this connection that they always associate the leaves,
if there be any, with the flower, for their
object is to present the whole beauty of
plant life. In this respect, as in many others,
their method differs from that pursued in
Western countries. Here we are apt to see
only the flower stems, heads, as it were, without body, stuck promiscuously into a vase.

When a tea-master has arranged a flower
to his satisfaction he will place it on the
tokonoma, the place of honour in a Japanese

room. Nothing else will be placed near it which might interfere with its effect, not even a painting, unless there be some special aesthetic reason for the combination. It rests there like an enthroned prince, and the guests or disciples on entering the room will salute it with a profound bow before making their addresses to the host. Drawings from master-pieces are made and published for the edification of amateurs. The amount of literature on the subject is quite voluminous. When the flower fades, the master tenderly consigns it to the river or carefully buries it in the ground. Monuments even are sometimes erected to their memory.

The birth of the Art of Flower Arrangement seems to be simultaneous with that of Teaism in the fifteenth century. Our legends ascribe the first flower arrangement to those early Buddhist saints who gathered the flowers strewn by the storm and, in their infinite solicitude for all living things, placed them in vessels of water. It is said that Soami, the great painter and connoisseur of the court of

Ashikaga-Yoshimasa, was one of the earliest
adepts at it. Juko, the tea-master, was one of
his pupils, as was also Senno, the founder of
the house of Ikenobo, a family as illustrious
in the annals of flowers as was that of the
Kanos in painting. With the perfecting of
the tea-ritual under Rikiu, in the latter part
of the sixteenth century, flower arrangement
also attains its full growth. Rikiu and his
successors, the celebrated Oda-Wuraku,
Furuta-Oribe, Koyetsu, Kobori-Enshiu, Kata-
giri-Sekishiu, vied with each other in form-
ing new combinations. We must remember,
however, that the flower worship of the tea-
masters formed only a part of their aesthetic
ritual, and was not a distinct religion by
itself. A flower arrangement, like the other
works of art in the tea-room, was subordi-
nated to the total scheme of decoration. Thus
Sekishiu ordained that white plum blossoms
should not be made use of when snow lay in
the garden. "Noisy" flowers were relentlessly
banished from the tea-room. A flower arrangement by a tea-master loses its signifi-

❄ FLOWERS ❄

cance if removed from the place for which it was originally intended, for its lines and proportions have been specially worked out with a view to its surroundings.

The adoration of the flower for its own sake begins with the rise of "Flower-Masters," toward the middle of the seventeenth century. It now becomes independent of the tea-room and knows no law save that the vase imposes on it. New conceptions and methods of execution now become possible, and many were the principles and schools resulting therefrom. A writer in the middle of the last century said he could count over one hundred different schools of flower arrangement. Broadly speaking, these divide themselves into two main branches, the Formalistic and the Naturalesque. The Formalistic schools, led by the Ikenobos, aimed at a classic idealism corresponding to that of the Kano-academicians. We possess records of arrangements by the early masters of this school which almost reproduce the flower paintings of Sansetsu and Tsunenobu. The Naturalesque school,

on the other hand, as its name implies, accepted nature as its model, only imposing such
modifications of form as conduced to the
expression of artistic unity. Thus we recognise in its works the same impulses which
formed the Ukiyoe and Shijo schools of
painting.

It would be interesting, had we time, to
enter more fully than is now possible into
the laws of composition and detail formulated by the various flower-masters of this
period, showing, as they would, the fundamental theories which governed Tokugawa
decoration. We find them referring to the
Leading Principle (Heaven), the Subordi-
nate Principle (Earth), the Reconciling Principle (Man), and any flower arrangement
which did not embody these principles was
considered barren and dead. They also dwelt
much on the importance of treating a flower
in its three different aspects, the Formal, the
Semi-Formal, and the Informal. The first
might be said to represent flowers in the state-
ly costume of the ballroom, the second in the

easy elegance of afternoon dress, the third in the charming deshabille of the boudoir.

Our personal sympathies are with the flower-arrangements of the tea-master rather than with those of the flower-master. The former is art in its proper setting and appeals to us on account of its true intimacy with life. We should like to call this school the Natural in contradistinction to the Natural-esque and Formalistic schools. The tea-master deems his duty ended with the selection of the flowers, and leaves them to tell their own story. Entering a tea-room in late winter, you may see a slender spray of wild cherries in combination with a budding camellia; it is an echo of departing winter coupled with the prophecy of spring. Again, if you go into a noon-tea on some irritatingly hot summer day, you may discover in the darkened cool-ness of the tokonoma a single lily in a hang-ing vase; dripping with dew, it seems to smile at the foolishness of life.

A solo of flowers is interesting, but in a concerto with painting and sculpture the

combination becomes entrancing. Sekishiu
once placed some water-plants in a flat re-
ceptacle to suggest the vegetation of lakes
and marshes, and on the wall above he hung
a painting by Soami of wild ducks flying in
the air. Shoha, another tea-master, combined
a poem on the Beauty of Solitude by the Sea
with a bronze incense burner in the form
of a fisherman's hut and some wild flowers
of the beach. One of the guests has recorded
that he felt in the whole composition the
breath of waning autumn.

Flower stories are endless. We shall re-
count but one more. In the sixteenth century
the morning-glory was as yet a rare plant
with us. Rikiu had an entire garden planted
with it, which he cultivated with assiduous
care. The fame of his convolvuli reached the
ear of the Taiko, and he expressed a desire to
see them, in consequence of which Rikiu
invited him to a morning tea at his house.
On the appointed day the Taiko walked
through the garden, but nowhere could he
see any vestige of the convolvulus. The

ground had been leveled and strewn with fine pebbles and sand. With sullen anger the despot entered the tea-room, but a sight waited him there which completely restored his humour. On the tokonoma, in a rare bronze of Sung workmanship, lay a single morning-glory—the queen of the whole garden!

In such instances we see the full significance of the Flower Sacrifice. Perhaps the flowers appreciated the full significance of it. They are not cowards, like men. Some flowers glory in death—certainly the Japanese cherry blossoms do, as they freely surrender themselves to the winds. Anyone who has stood before the fragrant avalanche at Yoshino or Arashiyama must have realised this. For a moment they hover like bejewelled clouds and dance above the crystal streams; then, as they sail away on the laughing waters, they seem to say: "Farewell, O Spring! We are on to Eternity."

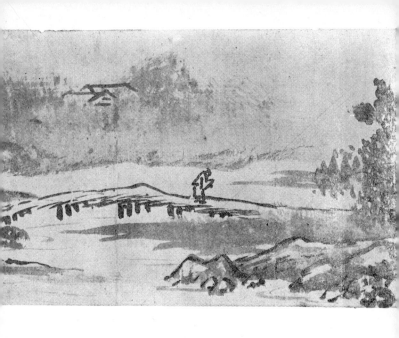

TEA-MASTERS

IN RELIGION the Future is behind us. In art the Present is the eternal. The tea-master held that real appreciation of art is only possible to those who make of it a living influence. Thus they sought to regulate their daily life by the high standard of refinement which obtained in the tea-room. In all circumstances serenity of mind should be maintained, and conversation should be so conducted as never to mar the harmony of the surroundings. The cut and colour of the dress, the poise of the body, and the manner of walking could all be made expressions of artistic personality. These were matters not to be lightly ignored, for until one has made himself beautiful he has no right to approach beauty. Thus the tea-master strove to be something more than the artist,—art itself. It was the Zen of aestheticism. Perfection is everywhere if we only choose to recognise it. Rikiu loved to quote an old poem which says: "To those who long only for flowers, fain would I show the full-blown spring which abides in the toiling buds of snow-covered hills."

Manifold indeed have been the contributions of the tea-masters to art. They completely revolutionised the classical architecture and interior decorations, and established the new style which we have described in the chapter of the tea-room, a style to whose influence even the palaces and monasteries built

after the sixteenth century have all been subject. The many-sided Kobori-Enshiu has left
notable examples of his genius in the Imperial villa of Katsura, the castles of Nagoya
and Nijo, and the monastery of Kohoan. All
the celebrated gardens of Japan were laid out
by the tea-masters. Our pottery would probably never have attained its high quality of
excellence if the tea-masters had not lent to
it their inspiration, the manufacture of the
utensils used in the tea-ceremony calling
forth the utmost expenditure of ingenuity on
the part of our ceramists. The Seven Kilns
of Enshiu are well known to all students of
Japanese pottery. Many of our textile fabrics
bear the names of tea-masters who conceived
their colour or design. It is impossible, indeed, to find any department of art in which
the tea-masters have not left marks of their
genius. In painting and lacquer it seems almost superfluous to mention the immense
service they have rendered. One of the greatest schools of painting owes its origin to the
tea-master Honnami-Koyetsu, famed also as

a lacquer artist and potter. Beside his works, the splendid creation of his grandson, Koho, and of his grand-nephews, Korin and Kenzan, almost fall into the shade. The whole Korin school, as it is generally designated, is an expression of Teaism. In the broad lines of this school we seem to find the vitality of nature herself.

Great as has been the influence of the tea-masters in the field of art, it is as nothing compared to that which they have exerted on the conduct of life. Not only in the usages of polite society, but also in the arrangement of all our domestic details, do we feel the presence of the tea-masters. Many of our delicate dishes, as well as our way of serving food, are their inventions. They have taught us to dress only in garments of sober colours. They have instructed us in the proper spirit in which to approach flowers. They have given emphasis to our natural love of simplicity, and shown us the beauty of humility. In fact, through their teachings tea has entered the life of the people.

Those of us who know not the secret of properly regulating our own existence on this tumultuous sea of foolish troubles which we call life are constantly in a state of misery while vainly trying to appear happy and contented. We stagger in the attempt to keep our moral equilibrium, and see forerunners of the tempest in every cloud that floats on the horizon. Yet there is joy and beauty in the roll of the billows as they sweep outward toward eternity. Why not enter into their spirit, or, like Liehtse, ride upon the hurricane itself?

He only who has lived with the beautiful can die beautifully. The last moments of the great tea-masters were as full of exquisite refinement as had been their lives. Seeking always to be in harmony with the great rhythm of the universe, they were ever prepared to enter the unknown. The "Last Tea of Rikiu" will stand forth forever as the acme of tragic grandeur.

Long had been the friendship between Rikiu and the Taiko-Hideyoshi, and high

the estimation in which the great warrior
held the tea-master. But the friendship of a
despot is ever a dangerous honour. It was an
age rife wth treachery, and men trusted not
even their nearest kin. Rikiu was no servile
courtier, and had often dared to differ in
argument with his fierce patron. Taking ad-
vantage of the coldness which had for some
time existed between the Taiko and Rikiu,
the enemies of the latter accused him of being implicated in a conspiracy to poison the
despot. It was whispered to Hideyoshi that
the fatal potion was to be administered to
him with a cup of the green beverage prepared by the tea-master. With Hideyoshi
suspicion was sufficient ground for instant
execution, and there was no appeal from the
will of the angry ruler. One privilege alone
was granted to the condemned—the honour
of dying by his own hand.

On the day destined for his self-immola-
tion, Rikiu invited his chief disciples to a last
tea-ceremony. Mournfully at the appointed
time the guests met at the portico. As they

look into the garden path the trees seem to
shudder, and in the rustling of their leaves
are heard the whispers of homeless ghosts.
Like solemn sentinels before the gates of
Hades stand the grey stone lanterns. A wave
of rare incense is wafted from the tea-room;
it is the summons which bids the guests to
enter. One by one they advance and take their
places. In the tokonoma hangs a kakemono,
—a wonderful writing by an ancient monk
dealing with the evanescence of all earthly
things. The singing kettle, as it boils over the
brazier, sounds like some cicada pouring forth
his woes to departing summer. Soon the host
enters the room. Each in turn is served with
tea, and each in turn silently drains his cup,
the host last of all. According to established
etiquette, the chief guest now asks permission to examine the tea-equipage. Rikiu
places the various articles before them with
the kakemono. After all have expressed admiration of their beauty, Rikiu presents one
of them to each of the assembled company
as a souvenir. The bowl alone he keeps.

"Never again shall this cup, polluted by the lips of misfortune, be used by man." He speaks, and breaks the vessel into fragments.

The ceremony is over; the guests with difficulty restraining their tears, take their last farewell and leave the room. One only, the nearest and dearest, is requested to remain and witness the end. Rikiu then removes his tea-gown and carefully folds it upon the mat, thereby disclosing the immaculate white death robe which it had hitherto concealed. Tenderly he gazes on the shining blade of the fatal dagger, and in exquisite verse thus addresses it:

"Welcome to thee,
O sword of eternity!
Through Buddha
And through Dharuma alike
Thou hast cleft thy way."

With a smile upon his face Rikiu passed forth into the unknown.

OKAKURA KAKUZO
A BIOGRAPHICAL SKETCH

OKAKURA KAKUZO
A BIOGRAPHICAL SKETCH

by Elise Grilli

ON DECEMBER 26, 1862, a second son was born to
Okakura Kanemon, in a merchant family of Yoko-
hama, and named Kakuzo. This was almost ten
years after the historic "black ships" of Commodore
Perry had forced open the ports of Japan, which
for two hundred and fifty years had been tightly
shut against the rest of the world. Japan was by
no means unanimous in welcoming this intrusion
on her national privacy. Bloody uprisings of em-
battled traditionalists had to be suppressed before
the innovators won out and, in 1868, placed upon
the throne an emperor who by fiat would turn a
medieval country into a modern nation, almost
overnight.

The new capital, Tokyo, and its seaport, Yoko-
hama, were the geographic centers of the national
transformation. Young Okakura Kakuzo, like
many other merchants' sons of the time, was raised
with a definite orientation toward the West. He

learned English in the home from infancy on, and then continued his linguistic studies at the newly established School for Foreign Studies in Tokyo. There he concentrated on English, as the key to the new world, and on Chinese, as the mother language of Japan's literary and artistic culture. This dualism of interests formed the central threads in the fabric of his life, finally becoming firmly twisted into a single cord when, precisely because he was able to absorb ancient ideas and express them in a new language, he became a link between the cultures of two hemispheres.

When Okakura entered the Tokyo Imperial University in 1877, he was directed to the study of law and political economy, but was thrown off his course through his encounter with Ernest Fenollosa. This American teacher had come to Japan as professor of political economy; then he added aesthetics to his work; and gradually he was drawn deeper and deeper into the study of Oriental arts. The relationship of teacher and student soon changed to one of fellow workers in a new task that was evolving under their very eyes.

The new political structure of Japan attempted a separation of church and state and severed the Buddhist temples and Shinto shrines from state protection. Numerous monasteries and religious institutions, financially hard pressed, threw open their ancient treasuries and tried to dispose of their

120

paintings and sculpture. Rabid innovators were proclaiming these historic arts as hopelessly out of fashion and all but worthless. Collections of many centuries were scattered, and what could not be readily sold was often broken or burned to make room for the new. In the orgy of foreignism that swept every corner of the nation's life, the arts of Japan seemed doomed to be swept aside and replaced by European models of a type generally considered academic and passé in their home countries.

This wholesale destruction of a nation's cultural heritage aroused to action a small group of Japanese artists and men of letters and a handful of foreigners who seemed more concerned about the fate of Japanese art than were many native hotheads. The nucleus of this movement emerged from the Imperial University in Tokyo, with Professors Morse and Fenollosa in the lead, and with Kano Hogai, of the ancient family of artists, to act as historic instructor. Fenollosa urged his wealthy friend, William Sturgis Bigelow, to buy up whatever of value was tossed on a careless market; this was to become the core of the great Oriental collection of the Boston Museum. Okakura Kakuzo and Baron Kuki were the most energetic Japanese workers in the group. All these men united to organize the Kanga-kai, the artists' association for the conservation of the Japanese painting tradition. Out of this beginning there later grew an art school, a national museum, and a Committee for the Protection of Cultural Properties.

These struggles of an emerging national art movement were described, after Fenollosa's death, in Mary Fenollosa's introduction to her husband's posthumously published *Epochs of Chinese and Japanese Art*. It is significant, however, that Okakura's name is never mentioned in these pages. He is referred to obliquely as one of the "two Japanese colleagues" who traveled with Fenollosa to Kyoto and Osaka for art research, and to Europe in 1886 for observation of Western methods of art education. After half a year in Europe the travelers passed through America on their way back to Japan.

The exact cause of the later split between Fenollosa and Okakura remains a mystery, but the general causes are not far to seek. Both men have been described as individualists; each was engulfed in the sense of his own importance in this special mission; and each was completely assured that his personal gifts were suited to this task. Both were also volubly emotional personalities, who approached the study of art with passionate intensity rather than with scholarly objectivity. Their mutual admiration and their respective need of each other's background could not prevent the clashes that were bound to flare up between two such men. And of no little importance was the final shift in their positions. The Japanese pupil, who had sat at the feet of the great foreign teacher during his university days, gradually moved up to the level of friend and companion. Finally, he may have felt that he understood Oriental art more profoundly than did the American, who, after all, had encountered Japanese art late in life and who brought no special training to this work.

The Japanese government proved to be even less grateful and tactful than Okakura. Fenollosa's influence was declining. The new students could not understand his lectures in English, for the linguistic training of the later Meiji era was no longer of the quality that had developed an Okakura into a bilingual writer. In 1890 Fenollosa returned to America, while Okakura was elevated to the position of principal of the newly established national art school. He was then only twenty-nine years of age.

Okakura's administration of the Tokyo Bijutsu Gakko (the school's name has since been changed to Geijutsu Daigaku) must have been very colorful. Ever dramatic, always the extrovert, Okakura verged almost on the theatrical when he designed for himself and for his students a uniform which he intended to be "Chinese Taoist," or roughly equivalent to the costume worn during the Nara period in Japan. From the faded images seen on old photographs, this costume consisted of a voluminous cloak of heavy homespun and a cap that was vaguely

of the T'ang period. Thus accoutered, the principal
of the school would arrive at the institution astride
a horse that really lent him the dignity of an
ancient feudal lord. When he ascended the lecture
platform, he strode about with thespian gestures
and completely magnetized his students with his
compelling enthusiasm, his clear grasp of the essence
of art, and his stentorian delivery. His surviving
students still grow incandescent when they recall
those days. Evidently his platform manner was
sufficiently eloquent to surmount any obstacles of
language and geography, for similar reactions
occurred among his listeners during numerous
lectures which Okakura later delivered in America.

Among the first pupils in the new government
art school were the highly gifted Yokoyama Taikan,
Shimomura Kanzan, and Hishida Shunso, who
were to develop into the leading artists of the
Japanese style during the next half century. Their
devotion to Okakura was to be lifelong. Since they
called him Tenshin, this may be the moment to
explain the name by which he is still known to
his countrymen. It has always been customary for
Japanese artists and writers to move through several
noms d'artiste before they settled on some specially
suitable one. This was true of Sesshu, of Korin, of
Hokusai, and remains the practice to this day. The
color and flavor of such names surpasses logical
meaningfulness, and they are not always translatable,

hinging as they do on the sound and aura that surround the Chinese ideograms which make up such names. In the case of Tenshin we have *ten*, meaning "heaven," and *shin*, meaning "heart." Make of that what you will. The implications are evidently transcendental and lyrical.

Despite the fervent devotion of his students and his staff, all did not go well at the school. The battle against the Europeanizing faction was by no means over. This question of *Nihonga* versus *Yoga*, or Japanese tradition in painting versus foreign trends, has not found a final solution to this day (although it has reached a mode of "peaceful co-existence"). Nor was this divergence of ideologies the only bone of contention. The young man who had risen so rapidly to a position of high governmental rank had outdistanced many of his former superiors. His arrogant and self-assured manner was hardly calculated to let these men overlook such slights. Cabals and intrigues sprang up all around him. The tension had been rising for a number of years and the final outbreak came through a series of accusations in anonymous letters calculated to discredit the school, its policies, and its leadership.

In 1898 Tenshin resigned from the school and about half of the faculty left with him. They immediately founded a dissident school and art association, entitled Nihon Bijutsu-in, with the program of continuing the protection of the grand

125

old tradition and its continued evolution into newer, living forms—a sort of renovation from within, aware of Western ideas but not subservient to them. Fenollosa, who had returned to Japan for a stay of two years, apparently bore no grudge and acted as critic for the first exhibition arranged by the Bijutsu-in, praising paintings by`Yokoyama Taikan and Shimomura Kanzan. Bigelow sent a gift of one thousand dollars to help the financial stabilization of the new group.

Two journeys to China and India confirmed in Okakura his ardent belief in the destiny of the East as a cultural and philosophical counterpoint to the rapidly spreading materialism of the West. During his trip to India in 1902 he met Rabindranath Tagore, and at once both men sensed in each other a kindred spirit. Tagore opened his hospitable home in Calcutta to the group of Japanese travelers, which included, beside Tenshin, the priest Oda Tokuma, of the Higashi Honganji Buddhist sect, and Hishida Shunso, a painter-pupil of the Bijutsu-in. The Indian poet-philosopher was then only one year older than Tenshin, and out of their many talks and exchanges of ideas Tenshin crystallized his essay on *The Ideals of the East*. This was to be Tenshin's first publication in English; it appeared in London in 1904, two years before the publication of *The Book of Tea*. A humbler and more material memento of the meeting with Tagore was the strange, tall cap which was given to the dramatic Japanese visitor by his Indian friend. It is this cap which Okakura wears on the portrait painted by Shimomura Kanzan (*see Frontispiece*).

The Bijutsu-in was still in financial straits and it was hoped to recoup its fortunes by the sale of some works of art in America. It was for this purpose that Tenshin started out for the United States, together with the painters Yokoyama Taikan, Hishida Shunso, and Rokkaku Shisui. Their first friendly encounter was with the American painter, John La Farge, who may have remembered Okakura from a brief journey which La Farge and Henry Adams had made to Japan in 1886. La Farge had maintained a steady interest in Japanese art and had witnessed its spread to the England of Whistler and the France of the impressionist painters. La Farge gave Okakura a letter of introduction to Mrs. Isabella Gardner, and when this "Queen of Boston" smiled upon the Japanese artists, their path in America grew noticeably easier. Mrs. Gardner was predisposed to accept them, for she had visited Japan as far back as 1882, when she and her wealthy husband journeyed around the world to ease their grief after the death of their child.

Boston, at that time, contained a small circle of art collectors, aesthetes, and philosophers who looked to the Far East as well as to Renaissance Italy for the subtleties of thought and the artistic refinements they felt lacking in their own America, which was then bent on geographic and material expansion. In 1903 Mrs. Gardner had opened her new home at Fenway Court, a transplanted Venetian palace that had been ten years in the building. Her enthusiasms were broad enough to include *quattrocento* Italian art, Oriental *objects d'art*, and John Singer Sargent. The eloquence and impressive presence of Tenshin made him a natural high priest of that small but recherché world in Boston.

The Japanese visitors, in their dignified garb, consisting of the ceremonial *hakama* skirt and *haori* coat of fine Japanese silk in deep, muted colors, made a welcome addition to the Boston scene. A favorite anecdote of Taikan's recounts an incident that occurred on one of their promenades through the streets of Boston. They were accosted by a cocky young man who asked: "What sort of 'nese are you people? Are you Chinese, or Japanese, or Javanese?" Whereto the quick-witted Tenshin retorted: "We are Japanese gentlemen. But what kind of 'key are you? Are you a Yankee, or a donkey, or a monkey?" In addition to revealing the barbed sharpness of his tongue, this tale attests to Tenshin's facility in thinking and speaking in English.

The exhibition and sale of Japanese paintings in New York and Boston (followed by an exhibit in London) was a great success and yielded enough financial returns to allow the younger travelers to return via Europe and to continue the Bijutsu-in in Japan, while Tenshin remained behind in America. In 1904, armed with letters of recommendation from Mrs. Gardner, he set out for the International Exposition of St. Louis, where he was to give a lecture at the International Conference of Culture and Literature. He had been asked to step in when the director of the Louvre Museum defaulted. Tenshin's lecture, entitled "Problems of Modern Painting," was received with great enthusiasm and was later reprinted in the *Quarterly Review*. It was on the strength of this favorable reaction, plus the power behind the throne which Mrs. Gardner exerted on his behalf, that Okakura was offered the position at the Boston Museum, first as Advisor and later as Curator of the Department of Chinese and Japanese Art. This work began in 1906 and was to continue until his death in 1913.

These years were by no means sedentary or confined to Boston. He traveled back and forth between America and Japan, making six journeys in all, some of them almost round-the-world trips, via Europe, Siberia, and China. On behalf of the Boston Museum he acquired works of art in India, China, and Japan, and he thus rounded out the fabulous acquisitions of the museum that had begun with the Fenollosa-Weld Collection, the Bigelow Collection, and, later, the Denman Ross Collection. As an

Oriental, Tenshin was able to penetrate into places in China that were entirely inaccessible to a Westerner. At times he could travel only in the disguise of full Chinese dress and pigtail. Here again his early studies of the Chinese language stood him in good stead; if there was some trace of a foreign accent in his Chinese speech—well, amidst the myriads of dialects that prevail in China, who was to detect a newly strange one?

His final trip to China, soon after the Revolution of 1912, is recorded in Tenshin's own words in the Boston Museum *Bulletin* of 1912. He contrasts the Chinese hoarding of art treasures with the Japanese dispersion that he had witnessed in his youth, in the early days after the Meiji Restoration. He must have searched China most assiduously to have found enough treasures to elicit the following tribute from Dr. Osvald Siren (Preface to his *Chinese Paintings in American Collections,* Paris, 1928):

"The number of pictures which he bought was by no means as large as that given by the various afore-mentioned donors, but their quality was of a kind that practically overshadowed all the earlier acquisitions. It was only through Okakura's purchases that the collection of Chinese paintings in the Boston Museum became the foremost of its kind in the Western world; thanks to his great knowledge of Eastern art and practical experience, he was better fitted than anyone else at the time to buy the right things for a museum that needed only the 'top pieces' in order to have the whole evolution of Chinese painting well represented."

Okakura also performed Herculean labors in the classification and arrangement of the accumulated treasures, some of which were still crated and stored until the new Oriental wing could be opened. This work was described in an article in the Museum *Bulletin,* that appeared (in December 1913) shortly after his death.

"The mere mechanical labor was far greater than any one man could attend to, and he secured the assistance of competent experts from Japan to classify the lacquers and the metal work, while he himself undertook the examination and cataloguing of paintings and sculptures. It was a matter of great interest to see how rapidly the systematic study of art in Japan along the lines of Western research had altered the standards of judgment in twenty years, especially in the matter of conventional attributions, many of which were completely reversed.... Okakura's work was untiring, incessant, and extended in many directions. He did a great deal to arouse the community to a realizing sense of what a wonderful treasure it possessed in the Japanese and Chinese collections."

It should be stressed that to the end Okakura Tenshin remained a man of two worlds. His work in America did not cut him off from his life in Japan. His family never accompanied him abroad and he continued to return to his wife and children who lived at Izura. In that tiny fishing hamlet the returning wanderer found relaxation with his friends, half of whom were local fishermen, while the other half included some of the most renowned artists of the day. There Langdon Warner also came to visit him, to ask his advice on questions of research, and to seal that warm friendship for Japan which led Professor Warner to intercede for Kyoto and Nara as "open cities," not to be bombed during the holocaust of World War II.

One of Tenshin's last public appearances—he was quite ill and feverish at the time—was in Kyoto, in August 1913, where he went as a representative of the Committee for the Protection of Cultural Properties. His impassioned talk on that occasion was, ironically enough, an urgent plea for the preservation of the fresco paintings in the Horyu-ji monastery of Nara, which dated back to the seventh or eighth century.

Tenshin died at Akakura hot springs in the Japanese Alps, on September 2, 1913. Some thirty-six years later, victims of a disastrous fire despite all the best efforts of men like Tenshin for the preservation of Japan's art treasures, the Horyu-ji frescoes were dead too.

REFERENCES

Carter, H.D. *Isabella Gardner at Fenway Court.*

Bulletin of the Museum of Fine Arts. Boston, December, 1913.

Kiyomi Rokuro. *Senkakusha Okakura Tenshin* (Okakura Tenshin the Pioneer). Tokyo, 1942.

Kiyomi Rokuro. *Tenshin Okakura Kakuzo* (Tenshin: Okakura Kakuzo). Tokyo, 1945.

Muraoka Hiroshi. Preface to *The Awakening of Japan* by Okakura. Tokyo, 1940.

New York Times, March 20, 1904. Press interview, with portraits of Taikan, Shunso and Shisui.

Saito Ryuzo. "Senkaku Okakura Tenshin" (Okakura Tenshin Pioneer). In *Nihon Rekishi* (Japanese History), Tokyo, January, 1955.

Shinsen Daijinmei Jiten (Newly Selected Biographical Dictionary). Tokyo, 1937.

Siren, Osvald. Introduction to *Chinese Paintings in American Collections.*

Wakimoto Tokuro and Ohta Nakai. "Taidan" (Conversation). In *Gasetsu,* Tokyo, 1941.

Personal recollections by Okakura Koshiro, Tenshin's grandson and teacher at Doshisha University, Kyoto; Saito Ryuzo, Director of Nihon Bijutsu-in, Ueno; Ueno Naoaki, President of Geijutsu University, Ueno; Wakimoto Tokuro, Head of the Library, Geijutsu University; and Yokoyama Taikan, the painter.